Peter H. Rolfs

Vegetable Growing in the South for Northern Markets

being concise directions for the preparation of the soil, use and amounts of

fertilizers, and the planting of vegetable crops to obtain the earliest vegetables

Peter H. Rolfs

Vegetable Growing in the South for Northern Markets
being concise directions for the preparation of the soil, use and amounts of fertilizers, and the planting of vegetable crops to obtain the earliest vegetables

ISBN/EAN: 9783337286941

Printed in Europe, USA, Canada, Australia, Japan

Cover: Foto ©Lupo / pixelio.de

More available books at **www.hansebooks.com**

VEGETABLE GROWING

IN THE

SOUTH

FOR

NORTHERN MARKETS.

BEING CONCISE DIRECTIONS FOR THE PREPARATION OF
THE SOIL, USE AND AMOUNTS OF FERTILIZERS, AND
THE PLANTING OF VEGETABLE CROPS TO OBTAIN
THE EARLIEST VEGETABLES;

ALSO THE

BEST METHODS OF PACKING FOR SHIPPING, THE RAISING
OF SEED FOR MARKET, AND PRESERVING IT
FOR HOME USE.

BY P. H. ROLFS, M. SC.,

*Professor of Horticulture in the Florida State Agricultural College;
Horticulturist to the Florida Agricultural Experiment Station;
Chairman of the Standing Committee on Insects, Florida
State Horticultural Society; Member of American
Pomological Society, etc.*

RICHMOND:
THE SOUTHERN PLANTER PUBLISHING COMPANY.
1896.

DEDICATED TO THE AUTHOR'S ELDER BROTHER,
WHOSE EARNEST EFFORTS, IN YEARS PAST.
PREPARED THE WAY FOR THIS PUBLICATION.

THE AUTHOR.

PREFACE.

VEGETABLE GROWING forms an important branch of horticulture for the South. Formerly the land produced an abundant crop with a minimum of labor and no fertilizer, but the land, except in the alluvial bottoms of large rivers, and in drained lakes, is rapidly becoming poor. This change in condition necessitates a change in the operations to produce a full crop. Besides producing a large crop, it is imperative that this crop shall be produced when the prices are highest. A difference of ten days in the maturing of a vegetable often turns the balance from a gain to a loss. In this book I teach the reader how to have vegetables mature for market from one to three weeks earlier than those of his neighbor, who plants by the old methods.

The amount of fertilizer wasted on many establishments would make a fair profit on the total investment. I have, therefore, made the matter of fertilizing a prominent subject in this discussion of each vegetable. This subject is the first that has to be encountered in progressive vegetable growing.

Finally, this book was first written as lectures to the classes in horticulture. These lectures were revised and, by the advice of friends, prepared for publication. Numerous letters have also been received, asking where a book on vegetable growing for this section could be obtained. The only accessible printed matter for this district are Experiment Station Bulletins and agricultural papers. While these treat the subject in a thorough and excellent way, they are only fragments on the subject. If it were for no other reason than to bring this material together into one accessible volume, I would be justified in having it published.

P. H ROLFS

CONTENTS.

SOIL 1
    Mechanical classification of — Composition of—Elements necessary to plant growth—Why land becomes poor.

WHAT IS FERTILIZING?.. 4

COMMERCIAL FERTILIZER..................................... 5
    Sources of Phosphoric Acid—Potash—Nitrogen.

MANURE... 9
    Compost—Muck.

PER CENTS OF FERTILIZER ELEMENTS................. 14

HOW TO COMPUTE THE AMOUNT OF FERTILIZER IN A GIVEN FORMULA................................ 15

PLANTS USED TO ENRICH THE SOIL..................... 17
    As a source of Nitrogen.

HOW TO TEST A FIELD... 19

ROTATION OF CROPS... 21

WEEDS... 23

WATER AND WATERING... 24

SEED GROWING... 26
    How to test the vitality of seed.

SEED SOWING.. 29
    How to test a machine—Selecting varieties—Quantity of seed required.

HOT BEDS.. 32
    Selection of a location—Construction—Using the manure.

PREPARING A COLD FRAME.................................... 36

PREPARATION OF A PLANT BED............................. 37

PREPARATION OF THE LAND.................................. 38
    Land well drained—Clear the land—Shall we plow deep?

NUMBER OF PLANTS PER ACRE.. 41
TRANSPLANTING... 42
MARKETING.. 44
    The packing house—How to make a crate.
MUSHROOMS... 48
    Preparation of the bed.
ASPARAGUS.. 51
    Preparation of the plot — Planting — Cutting—Bunching and crating — Marketing — Blanching—Raising plants—Canning—Varieties—Fertilizer.
RHUBARB... 57
    Planting—Varieties—Fertilizer—Cultivation—Marketing—Forcing.
LETTUCE.. 61
    Plant bed—Preparing the field—Cultivating—Fertilizer formula—Varieties—Marketing—Raising seed.
ENDIVE.. 65
    Fertilizer formula.
CHICORY... 67
SPINACH.. 68
    Fertilizer formula.
BORECOLE KALE.. 71
CELERY... 72
    Soil—Preparation of the soil—Seed sowing—Transplanting. The new celery culture—Irrigation—Marketing—Preparing for market—Varieties—Fertilizer formula.
CELERIAC... 85
CABBAGE.. 86
    Plant bed—Varieties—Sowing the seed—Soil—Fertilizer formula—Fertilizer amounts—Planting and cultivating. Preparing for market—Marketing.
SPROUTS.. 91
CAULIFLOWER... 92
    Seed sowing—Soil—Setting out—Cultivation—Cutting—Crating—Varieties—Fertilizer formula.

BROCOLI.. 97
COLLARDS... 99
    Fertilizer formula.
KOHL-RABI... 101
ONION.. 102
    Soil—Preparing the land—Seed—Seed bed—Time to sow—
    Fertilizing—Fertilizer formula—Amounts of fertilizer—
    Setting out—Cultivation—The old plan—Curing the crop.
    Crating—Raising onions from sets—Varieties—Resumé.
LEEK.. 115
    Fertilizer.
GARLIC.. 117
CHIVES.. 117
TOBACCO... 118
    Varieties—Raising the seedlings—Transplanting—Fertilizer
    formula—Fertilizer amounts—Preparation of the land.
    Cultivating—Topping and suckering—Cutting—Hauling.
    Curing barns—Curing—Stripping and sorting.
PARSLEY... 125
    Varieties.
CRESS.. 127
NASTURTIUMS... 128
GLOBE ARTICHOKE.. 129
TOMATO.. 131
    Hot beds—Cold frames—Seed bed—Fertilizer formula—
    Fertilizer amounts—Varieties — Seed — Transplanting—
    Soil and location—Preparing the land—Setting out—
    Cultivating—Pruning—Staking—Trellising—Picking—
    Packing—Sorting—Summer and Fall crop—Saving seed.
    Canning.
EGG PLANT... 150
    Varieties—Hot beds and cold frames—Using flower pots—
    Soil and preparation—Fertilizer formula—Cultivation—
    Gathering—Marketing—Seed saving.
PEPPERS.. 159
    Varieties — Fertilizer formula — Fertilizer amounts—Hot
    beds and cold frames—Soil and preparation—Cultivating.
    Marketing—Saving seed.

OKRA 164
    Varieties.
CUCUMBER 167
    Soil and preparation—Cultivating—Picking and packing. Saving seed—Varieties—Fertilizer.
MUSK MELONS 175
    Soil and preparation—Varieties—Fertilizer formula—Fertilizer amounts—Planting and cultivating—Marketing—Saving seed.
GHERKINS 178
SQUASHES 179
    Selecting the soil—Fertilizer formula—Fertilizer amounts. Varieties—Planting—Cultivating—Marketing.
PUMPKINS 184
WATER MELONS 185
    Soil—Fertilizer formula—Fertilizer amounts—Varieties—Planting—Cultivating—Marketing—Saving seed.
GOURD 189
ENGLISH PEA 190
    Fertilizer formula—Fertilizer amounts.
BEAN 192
    BUSH BEAN—Varieties—Soil—Fertilizer formula—Planting and cultivating—Preparing for market—Harvesting.
    POLE BEAN—Varieties.
PEANUT 198
    Soil and preparation—Planting—Cultivating - Harvesting. Varieties—Fertilizer formula—Fertilizer amounts.
GOOBER 205
IRISH POTATO 206
    Soil and preparation—Seed—Planting—Fertilizer—Fertilizer formula—Fertilizer amounts—Cultivation—Harvesting—Storing—General Remarks—Varieties—Second Crop.
JERUSALEM ARTICHOKE 215
CHUFA 216

SWEET POTATO 217
   Soil—Propagation—Preparation of the land and transplanting — Cultivation — Fertilizer formula — Fertilizer amounts—Storing—Varieties—Uses—Cost of producing. Points to be improved upon.

YAM 225

RADISH 226
   Soil and preparation — Fertilizer formula — Fertilizer amounts—Varieties—Sowing and cultivating—Marketing—Seed raising.

BEET 230
   Soil and preparation—Fertilizer formula—Varieties—Seeding and cultivating—Marketing.

TURNIP 234
   Soil and preparation — Fertilizer formula — Fertilizer amounts—Varieties—Planting and cultivating—Marketing.

RUTA BAGA 237

CARROT 238
   Soil and preparation — Fertilizer formula — Fertilizer amounts—Varieties—Sowing and cultivating—Marketing.

PARSNIPS 241
   Soil and preparation — Fertilizer formula — Fertilizer amounts—Varieties—Sowing and cultivating.

SALSIFY 243

HORSE RADISH 244

VEGETABLE GROWING IN THE SOUTH
FOR NORTHERN MARKETS.

SOIL.

The earthy matter in which plants grow is commonly known as soil; it is more or less organic matter intermixed with finely pulverized rock.

The thin upper stratum in which plants grow is all that we are interested in for the present. The dark color in this stratum is due to the oxidation of the vegetable matter here present. The main source of oxygen is from the air. The portion of the soil that is dark is usually called the *soil*, and that immediately below it has been designated the *subsoil*. The soil is usually the more fertile, especially in the South; in some of the alluvial bottoms the soil is of the same consistency for a considerable depth.

The black vegetable mold in the soil we are used to call *humus* is an important factor. In it is contained mineral matter once the body of a rock and some decomposing vegetable matter, in a good condition to be again taken up by other plants. Besides the food for plants it keeps the soil in good condition for plant-growth. A sandy soil, rich in humus, can stand a drouth much better than where the humus is wanting, but unless there is a more or less compact stratum (subsoil) below, much of the fertilizer is carried off by the frequent rains and the land will always be poor.

MECHANICAL CLASSIFICATION OF SOILS.

Owing to the large per cent. of sand in many soils and its presence in all, it has been suggested that they be classified according to the amount of it they contain. Under this classification we are acquainted with the following divisions:

1. Pure clay, from which no sand can be removed by washing.
2. Strong clay, from which as much as 5 to 20 per cent. of sand can be separated.
3. Clay loam, when washing will remove 20 to 40 per cent. of sand.
4. Loam, when the land contains as much as 40 to 70 per cent. of sand.
5. Sandy loam, from which 70 to 90 per cent. of sand can be separated.
6. Light sand, containing more than 90 per cent. of sand.

When soil is found to contain a per cent. of carbonate of lime it is said to be *calcareous* or *marly* soil.

When a large per cent. of vegetable matter is present it is usually called *muck* or vegetable mold.

COMPOSITION OF THE SOILS.

Soils that are in good condition for raising crops are made up of fourteen or fifteen elements. In all, there are nearly seventy elements that may occur; but as only about fifteen of these enter into the question of plant economy, we need not regard the other fifty-five.

ELEMENTS NECESSARY TO PLANT-GROWTH.

The essential elements are oxygen, hydrogen, nitrogen, potassium, carbon, silicon, sulphur, phosphorus, chlorin, sodium, calcium, magnesium, aluminum and iron. Oxygen, hydrogen, nitrogen and carbon are derived directly from the air and constitute 95 per cent. to 99 per cent. of the weight of the plants. While these four elements are derived from the air, it should not be understood that they are usually taken directly from it by the plant, nor do they enter the plant in the condition of a simple element. Some plants that belong to the pea family are able, under certain conditions, to assimilate more or less nitrogen directly from the air, but the other three elements find their way into the plants through the soil. Because the above named elements make up so much of the weight, it should not be inferred that the other ten or eleven elements that are derived from the soil are of only minor importance. Although their combined weight is only from one to five per cent., the absence of any one of these may materially interfere with the growth of the plant.

WHY LAND BECOMES POOR.

It will be clear from what has been said that if crops are repeatedly removed from the soil, some element or elements will become exhausted, or, as we ordinarily say, the land becomes poor.

Different crops do not remove an equal amount of the elements, and even different specimens of the same crop vary considerably in the amount of any one element that they take up from the soil. Some plants take a great deal of nitrogen from the soil and return only a portion of it; others take only a small amount of nitrogen from the soil and give much back; the former make land poorer, the latter make it richer in nitrogen. The same is true in regard to plants using potash and phosphoric acid. When a piece of land becomes tired of one crop, it is often able to produce some other in fair quantity. To keep soil in such condition that it will produce a crop in paying quantities, we must keep the before named fifteen elements present in sufficient quantity—we must fertilize.

WHAT IS FERTILIZING?

Three of the essential plant elements are oftener wanting than any other; these are potash, nitrogen, and phosphoric acid.

They play such an important part in the plant economy, and are present in such varying quantities, and so often one or more of them is present in deficient quantities, that we look upon them as the essential elements, though they are not more necessary to the plant's welfare than some other elements. A deficiency of any one will cause the plants to look sickly, and make them a fit subject for insect and fungoid attacks, to which they readily succumb. If a field has been producing good crops for a number of years and then gradually fails, it is a pretty fair indication that some form of food for that crop is becoming exhausted, and we must either stop growing that crop on that soil or in some way supply the wanting plant foods. This is accomplished by using either home-made or commercial fertilizers.

COMMERCIAL FERTILIZER.

Any substance that will supply the deficient element or elements to the soil, in such a form that it is available to the crop to be produced, is considered a fertilizer. It is not uncommon to find an element in the soil in sufficient quantity, but in such a form that the crop cannot make use of it; in other words, the element is not available.

COMPLETE FERTILIZER.

A fertilizer that contains all three (nitrogen, potash and phosphoric acid) elements is said to be complete. The amount of any of the elements vary with the different brands and the different crops for which they are to be used. The amount of any element in a special fertilizer is governed by the amount of that element removed from the soil by that particular crop.

An incomplete fertilizer is one which is wanting in any one or more of the fertilizing elements. These are known either by the single element which they contain, as potash, muriate of potash, nitrate of soda, etc., or by some trade name, as kainit, blood and bone, guano, etc.

Any one who uses a large quantity of fertilizer will find it profitable to buy the simple fertilizers and mix them to suit the particular crop. When only a few tons are to be used, it is usually not profitable to mix the fertilizer at home. A few words in regard to the source of the fertilizer elements will be of value to us.

SOURCES OF PHOSPHORIC ACID.

A source of great commercial importance of this fertilizer element is the phosphate rock of Florida and South Carolina This rock contains a varying quantity of phosphoric acid, and it is necessary to make an analysis of it before one can know its value. The natural rock gives up the element slowly, so it is necessary to grind and treat it chemically to make the phosphoric acid available. In this condition, it is known as "acid phosphate," or "superphosphate."

BONES AS A SOURCE OF PHOSPHORIC ACID.

A second source of considerable commercial importance is the reduced bones from various animals. Before the discovery of the phosphate rock, this was a very important source; while the price of ground bone for fertilizer has not declined very much as a result of the discovery of rock phosphate, it has not increased as it otherwise would have. In their natural state, bones yield phosphoric acid but slowly, but, being crushed and treated with chemicals, they can be made to yield it up rapidly and become available in a short time. A vegetable grower having several tons of bones could make it profitable to change the insoluble phosphate of lime to a soluble form, which is usually called phosphoric acid. The best way to proceed is to grind the bones to meal; place about forty pounds of this meal in a wooden tub, containing thirty pounds of water; then add thirty pounds of sulphuric acid of a specific gravity of 1.7. Much less water could be used, but this quantity will enable one to mix the acid and bones more evenly. The essential part of the bones is the phosphate of lime, and, as before mentioned, this is insoluble, or, at best, only a small portion of it will go into solution. Now, when the sulphuric acid is supplied, it becomes a superphosphate, or acid phosphate; some people call it phosphoric acid, but the chemists object to this term because it is incorrectly used. This superphosphate is readily dissolved by water, and in such a state can be taken up and used by plants. After the sulphuric acid has put all the bone into solution, the material should be a more or less homogeneous sticky mass. Of course this could not be applied to a field readily, so it must be mixed with some drying material, as dry sand. Ashes or lime should not be used as drying material, because these are liable to revert the phosphate of lime to the insoluble form again. Generally, it will be found cheaper to buy the superphosphate than to buy the materials and prepare it.

The packing-houses and slaughter houses collect the bones and harder portion of refuse to grind up for fertilizer. When considerable blood is mixed with this bone meal, it goes under the name of blood and bone. The bones and refuse of fish in large fisheries, also the carcasses of worthless fish, are used for this important element of plant food. Thousands of tons of these forms of phosphoric acid are used yearly as fertilizer in the South.

POTASH.

In nature this usually occurs as a chloride (muriate), a sulphate, or a carbonate. It is very widely distributed, occurring in all parts of the world, and is one of the fertilizer ingredients that is left after plants are burned; in other words, it is one of the main ingredients of the ash of plants. Besides this general distribution, it also occurs in large bodies in parts of the earth. One of the largest and most important of these is located in Stassfurt, Germany, where it is mined much as salt is in the other portions of Europe. In this place it occurs as a sulphate mixed with common salt and other ingredients, and imported to this country under the name of kainit. When refined, it is sold on our market as muriate of potash or sulphate of potash, as the case may be.

NITROGEN.

In its natural state nitrogen occurs as an atmospheric gas, and as such it is not available as a fertilizer. When the term is used in speaking of a fertilizer, we simply mean that it is in some combination with other elements that hold it in the form of a solid.

The different forms in which nitrogen occurs as a fertilizer are : First, as organic matter, either vegetable or animal ; *e. g.*, tobacco stems, cotton-seed meal, dried blood and tankage. Second, as nitrates ; *e. g.*, nitrate of soda, nitrate of potash, etc. Third, in the form of ammonia compounds ; *e. g.*, sulphate of ammonia. In the reports of fertilizers, when the amount is given, it is intended to imply how much of it would be present if it were in the form of a gas.

MANURE.

This term is used for all forms of decomposed vegetable matter in barn-yards; whether it be animal excrement or other decomposed vegetable matter. Its value varies greatly, not only as to its source, but also as to the manner in which it is kept. When it is kept in the usual way it is worth from $2.00 to $4.00 per ton. About 60 to 80 per cent. of the whole weight is water; 9 to 15 pounds of it is nitrogen; 9 to 15 pounds of potash, and 4 to 9 pounds of phosphoric acid. From these variations it is plain that it is difficult to state just how much it is worth. If the manure has decomposed in the open air, there is danger of the rain having washed out much of the potash, and the nitrogen having passed off as a gas into the atmosphere. Manure that is to be kept for some time should be under a roof where the rain cannot wash out any of the soluble fertilizer. It should be kept from becoming too hot by being forked over or stirred in some way, or by using water when becoming dry. While the essential elements in the barn-yard manure may not equal those of a commercial fertilizer, it adds the important factor of humus to the soil, thus improving its mechanical condition.

COMPOST.

It has long been known that decomposing vegetable or animal matter causes plants to grow luxuriantly; but, at the same time, the plants are liable to be unfruitful. This is due to an over-abundance of nitrogenous matter. If, to this decomposing organic matter, potash and phosphoric acid be added to make a complete fertilizer, plants do not become "over grown." The amount of potash and phosphoric acid to be added is learned by experience. Such a mixture is called a compost. The term is often applied to a decomposing heap of organic matter, and also applied to such heaps when land plaster has been added; but we shall restrict the term compost to decomposed organic matter, to which enough commercial fertilizer elements have been added to make a complete fertilizer.

On any farm, garden or other places where lines of horticulture or agriculture are carried on, a good deal of coarse and refuse material can be collected without making a special effort. All offal, as vegetable refuse, kitchen slops, wash-water or soap-suds, the dung of domestic animals, bits of wood, in fact, anything of animal or vegetable origin may be used in this way. The best way to dispose of an animal that has died on the farm is to use it in the compost heap. When any odor is escaping from the compost heap or bin, we may be sure that valuable fertilizer is escaping; this may be arrested by mixing with the compost two or three bushels of land plaster to a cart-load of material. If land plaster is not at hand, two or three inches of moist dirt thrown over the pile will arrest the escaping nitrogen. The decomposition of material may be hastened by adding night soil or undecomposed manure, but it should be distributed evenly throughout the entire mass.

By the proper use of fresh manure, a compost may be prepared that will be ready for use in four or five weeks.

If any one wishes to compost material rapidly, the following general directions will be found of service. Have on hand about four barrels of concentrated manure, such as pure hen manure, cow manure, horse manure, or night soil; about five bushels of land plaster. This will be found to be enough to decompose a ton of dry and about eight tons of green matter. Place about six inches of muck on the bottom of the compost shed and wet it down thoroughly. Then put in a layer of six or eight inches of material to be decomposed; then add a thin layer of concentrated manure; then put another layer of rough matter, and follow with a layer of concentrated material, and so on till the required amount of material has been used. The body of the material should be made completely wet; if this is not done it is liable to "burn" and lose one of the important elements of plant food—nitrogen. Finally, mix the land plaster with enough fresh earth or thoroughly decomposed muck to cover the whole about eight inches thick. The muck in the bottom will catch any surplus moisture and save a waste of soluble fertilizer. The concentrated manure furnishes the germs that set up decay, the water distributes these germs and gives them a necessary moisture, while the land plaster arrests any escaping gases and holds them in an available form. Land plaster may be added to each layer of the compost to take up any gas as it is formed. The time required for decomposition depends very largely on the amount of concentrated material used and the completeness of the mixing with the coarse stuff. Caution should be exercised to keep the pile moist, but not wet; if it is so wet that liquid can be pressed out of it by squeezing it in the hand, water must be withheld for several days; when no more moisture can be pressed out, water may again be applied. Often the process of decaying goes on too rapidly; in such a case much of the nitrogen may be lost. This is made apparent by the rising of steam or the sending off of ammonia gas, so easily detected by the nostrils. If the overheating is due to the want of water, it may be corrected by supplying the needed moisture, but sometimes it is necessary to fork the pile over to correct the temperature. After a little practice, one is able to prepare a heap so it will not have to be disturbed until it is to be applied to the field.

If one has determined for what crop the compost is to be used, the proper amount of commercial fertilizer may be added as the pile is prepared, otherwise this must be added when the compost is to be used. There are two advantages in the use of compost: First, it improves the mechanical condition of the soil; Second, the soluble chemical fertilizer is taken up by the vegetable matter and held in suspension much as a sponge holds water, thus keeping the rains from leaching it out of the soil, and as it is in a more finely divided state, the growing plants can absorb it with greater facility. In preparing compost, it must be done under shelter to keep the water from washing out the soluble fertilizer.

MUCK.

There has been so much said and so much written on this subject, and so many heated discussions engaged in, that the very mention of the term causes a ripple of merriment in the Florida State Horticultural Society. Much of the discussion would not have occurred if the arguments had been confined closely to the question at issue. Usually the only fertilizing element present in muck is nitrogen, and this varies widely in different samples, from one per cent. in a poor grade to six or seven in the best. However, if we are sure that our soil needs this element, nitrogen, and wants humus, all that we have to do is to get the per cent. present in the supply and calculate whether it is cheaper to use this source or to get it from some other form. The later portion of the problem cannot be worked out so easily; general common sense will aid us much in this. The particular crop to be grown on that piece of land will have much to do with the advisability of hauling muck. It is generally conceded that muck is an important source of nitrogen and will prove of great value where properly and intelligently used.

Besides its good quality as a fertilizer, muck in a dry and powdered form makes one of the best absorbents and disinfectants. It is a first class absorbent in horse stables, cattle sheds and similar places. The moisture is taken up quickly and the odor arrested. The importance of saving the urine of animals is usually overlooked largely because there seems to be no handy way of saving it. By using dry muck it is as easily handled as commercial fertilizer.

Per Cents. of Fertilizer Elements.

Table giving the approximate amounts of different fertilizer elements in various substances used in the South.

Materials used for Nitrogen.	Nitrogen, per cent.	Ammonia Equivalent, per cent.	Potash, K_2O per cent.	Available Phosphoric Acid, per cent.	Insoluble Phosphoric Acid, per cent.
Cotton-seed meal	6–7	7–8	1	2	
Dried blood	10–15	12–18			
Dried fish scraps	7–8	8–10		6–8	
Guano	7–8	8–10	2–4	5 8	
Muck, good	1–3	1–4			
Nitrate of soda	15–16	18–20			
Tobacco stems	2–3	3–4	5–8	1	
Sulphate of ammonia	19–22	23–26			
Materials used for Potash.					
Cotton-seed hull ashes			15–25	6–8	
Kainit			8–9		
Muriate of potash (80 to 85 per cent.)			50		
Nitrate of potash	13–14	16–18	43 44	2	
Saw Palmetto ashes (unleached)			35–40		
Sulphate of potash (high grade)			48 51		
Sulphate of potash and magnesia			26–28		
Tobacco stems	2–3	3–4	5–8		
Wood ashes (leached)			1–3		
Wood ashes (unleached)			4–8		
Used for Phosphoric Acid.					
Acid phosphate				10–14	1–3
Bone meal				4–8	16–17
Bone meal (glue f'ct'y)					20–22
Bone meal (dissolved)				12–18	2 8
Florida rock					25–35
Florida soft phosphate					18–20
Guano	7–8	8–10	2–4	5–8	
South Carolina phosphate					25–30

How to Compute the Amount of Fertilizer in a Given Formula.

It is very important that we should be able to compute the amount of any essential fertilizer element contained in a certain formula. Unless we are able to find this out, we cannot make an intelligent use of the substance. Very often a high grade and a low grade fertilizer can be obtained on the same market—then it is very essential that the relative values of these shall be obtained in order that we buy intelligently. It does not concern us further than the difference in handling, whether we have to use a half ton or a ton of fertilizer to get the requisite amount of an essential element; so, if we can get the requisite amount of a certain element in low grade fertilizer for enough less to pay for its handling and something over, that will be the preferable kind to buy. To illustrate: Suppose we have a fertilizer containing 10 per cent. available phosphoric acid, 8 per cent. potash, and 6 per cent. nitrogen. A ton of this gives 200 pounds (10 per cent. of 2000 pounds a ton) phosphoric acid, 160 pounds potash, and 120 nitrogen. The remainder is usually some harmless earthy substance. Now, suppose there is another fertilizer on the market that contains 6 per cent. of available phosphoric acid, 6 per cent. of potash, and 4 per cent. of nitrogen. A ton will give us 120 pounds phosphoric acid, 120 pounds potash, and 80 pounds of nitrogen. The value of different fertilizing elements varies from year to year. We will use figures that are approximately correct. If nitrogen is worth 12 cents a pound, available phosphoric acid 10 cents, and potash 6 cents, we will have the following comparison in values of the respective formulas:

First Formula.

200 pounds phosphoric acid, 10c	$20 00
160 pounds potash, 6c.	9 60
120 pounds nitrogen, 12c, ...	14 40
Total.	$44 00

Second Formula.

120 pounds phosphoric acid, 10c............	$12 00
120 pounds potash, 6c..	7 20
80 pounds nitrogen, 12c.	9 60
Total....	$28 80

This shows that the former fertilizer is worth $15.20 more per ton than the latter, but suppose that the latter fertilizer were offered you at the depot for $26, then it is necessary to decide whether you make anything by buying the cheaper and have the extra hauling and handling. There is still another point to be considered : if the latter fertilizer costs $28.80 per ton, a pound will cost $.0144; $44 (the price of the former) will buy 3,055 pounds. Of this, 183¼ pounds (6 per cent. of 3,055 pounds) are phosphoric acid, 183¼ pounds are potash, and 122¼ pounds nitrogen. If the latter formula is chosen at the price ($28.80) given for its value, one obtains 16⅞ pounds phosphoric acid less, 23¼ pounds potash more, and 2⅕ pounds nitrogen more for the same money than by buying the former.

PLANTS USED TO ENRICH SOIL.

During the year, rain falls on the land leeching out much soluble fertilizer, unless there be some way of holding it in the soil. Fertilizer must be in a soluble condition before plants can appropriate it. Now, if there are no plants present to appropriate this soluble fertilizer, it is plain that the rain will carry this portion out of the soil into the water-ways; but if plants use it at once, when it becomes available, it remains on the land. When these plants decay, they return this stored up food and humus to the soil.

PLANTS AS A SOURCE OF NITROGEN.

The source of nitrogen, primarily, is the air; it enters the plants in different ways; some take it up from the soil, and a few are known to take it from the air directly. Plants that do not appropriate it from the air are still important conservators of nitrogen, in that they take it up from the soil and keep it from wasting, and at the end of their life they give it back. This class of plants cannot give to the soil more nitrogen than they draw out, but they can conserve it for future plants. Besides this, they pile up the other soluble elements of plant-food. The nitrogen-assimilating plants store up varying amounts of this element and give it to the soil, thus actually adding to the supply of this important element and keeping the other elements from wasting. By producing a crop on land for a number of years, and utilizing it carefully, the land becomes richer until finally it will grow full crops.

The best plants for green manuring or soiling now in cultivation in the South are cow-peas (*Dolichos sp.*)

and beggar-weed (*Desmodium tortuosum*). The latter of these has some points of advantage over the former; one of the main points to be considered is that root-knot (*Heterodera radicicola*) does not attack it as severely as the former. This is quite important, as it means failure to follow cow-peas with a crop attacked by root-knot if the disease is in the field.

As to the manner of using these plants, there is some diversity of opinion. In clay soil, the plants may be plowed under in the green state, but on sandy soils it will not be found practicable. Dr. Stubbs, Director of the Louisiana Agricultural Experiment Station, says that in the South it is a detrimental practice, and that the green manure should be allowed to rot before it is plowed under. The decomposition of the green matter is said to create a ferment in the soil detrimental to crops that may follow.

HOW TO TEST A FIELD.

In some European countries where horticulture and agriculture are more advanced than they are are in this country, the tillers of the soil have certain test plants; that is, certain quick growing plants, as oats, are planted and their color and growth watched, and from these the conditions of the soil interpreted. In this way the soil is tested and it is learned just what elements are wanting to make the crop remunerative. In this country the tests have not been thorough enough nor continued long enough to make them of value. However, certain good horticulturists can tell to some extent by the condition of the foliage what is wanted by certain plants. To obtain information of this kind, it requires careful attention to various crops grown on different grades of land whose composition is known and to keep careful notes on these for a long series of years. Unfortunately, there are so many other conditions that come in to vary the test that most people become impatient before any definite conclusion could be reached.

Our sandy soil is unusually well adapted to work of this kind, as so much of it is deficient in all the essential fertilizing elements. Any one raising vegetables could withhold one of the three necessary fertilizers for a series of years on as many different plots as there are elements and thereby learn the effect of such treatment, and then by noting the color of the foliage, form of growth and other characters, learn to interpret these when observed in other fields.

To test a field to learn whether it really needs all the elements of a complete fertilizer, we may proceed as follows: Choose four rows of, say, tomatoes that run across a typical portion of the field and withhold from these one of the fertilizer elements, we will say nitrogen; then treat four rows the same as the rest of the field; then take the next four rows and withhold the potash from these; now treat four rows with the usual fertilizer; then take a third set of four rows and withhold the phosphoric acid from these. While the tests are being prepared, a number of strong stakes are made ready to mark off each plot by driving them securely into the ground at the first row of each test. If a second dressing of fertilizer is given to the crop, care must be exercised not to apply the element that was withheld when the first dressing was made. In making such a test it is almost useless to use only one or two rows, as the plants will draw their supply of the wanting element from the neighboring row. After such a test has been made, the crop from this portion should be measured carefully and compared with that of the neighboring rows. Now, if the first four rows show a decidedly poorer crop and the other two sets of four rows are of an average production, it is plain that the field needs nitrogen, but if the first and third sets of four rows have fallen off, the field needs nitrogen and phosphoric acid and not potash. There are several gardeners in the South that have saved money by testing their fields in this way.

Another way that has been employed, but one that does not tell quite as much, is to use the plots in the same way described above, but in the place of using two elements, use only one; for example, choose four rows and fertilize these with a nitrogenous fertilizer, containing neither potash nor phosphoric acid; then leave four rows for a check; then treat four rows with phosphoric acid, etc. On vegetables either of these tests are easily performed, but on fruit trees the results are so slow in making themselves manifest that it has not proven a success.

A portion of our land is not benefitted by the addition of potash, but nitrogen and phosphoric acid are nearly always deficient. Nitrogen is usually present in sufficient quantities in muck land, but it often needs lime to put it into fit condition for plant food.

ROTATION OF CROPS.

When a certain crop has been grown for a number of years in the same field, it often occurs that the yield decreases with each successive harvest, until finally an amount scarcely more than the seed used is returned. When a different crop is planted on such land it usually yields a paying crop, and after a number of years the original crop can be again grown with a profit. This phenomenon has given rise to the belief by some people that the first crop put something in the soil that was detrimental to itself; others held that there was something taken out of the soil that was afterwards restored. The latter, we have seen, were nearer the truth than the former. There are crops, however, that grow "tired" of a certain piece of land, or rather, the land grows "tired" of a certain crop. Some of these instances cannot be explained by the exhaustion of certain elements, but something else seems to be the cause. Certain pieces of land in Germany grew tired of growing beets, and it was called ruben-mude (beet-tired); after growing certain other crops on this land, it would again produce beets in the same quantity. Later investigation showed that this "beet-tired" was due to the presence of a microscopic worm closely related to the one that causes root-knot on our vegetables.

Certain crops are able to grow repeatedly on the same land and not cause any falling off in quantity or quality of the yield. For example, in an onion raising district a certain piece of land has grown more than thirty crops of onions, and the plot is preferred to-day to any of the surrounding land that was just as good formerly. Doctors Lawes and Gilbert grew wheat on the same plot for twenty consecutive years, and at the end of this time the land seemed fully as good for wheat as it was at the beginning of the experiment.

It is always a good practice, however, to change the crop grown in any field from year to year. In making changes of crops, they should be as different as possible. It is well to plant a field that has just had a good green soiling with some gross feeding crop, as the small grains or corn, and then to follow this with vegetables. To follow a crop of egg-plant with a crop of tomatoes could hardly have the force of rotation, in as much as the plants use about the same fertilizer and harbor the same insects; cabbage following cauliflower could not be considered a rotation for the same reason, but cabbage following tomatoes would make a good rotation.

WEEDS.

If we accept the definition, a weed is a plant out of place, almost any plant may become a weed. On the other hand, almost every weed can become an economic plant. Some one has wittily said that "the weed is the devil's flower." Most weeds certainly play mischief with a crop; they are ever present, springing up, it seems, spontaneously to take up the available fertilizer that was intended for the crop, thus leaving the young seedlings in a sickly and weak condition, unfit to combat with insects and other diseases.

Dr. B. D. Halsted, Horticulturist of New Jersey Experiment Station, has shown very clearly that weeds harbor diseases of crops. Some of the plant diseases are carried through the winter by weeds which nourish the spores that attack the crop in the spring. Other weeds act simply as harbors of insects, which leave the weed as soon as more refined food can be found. Poke weed is a prolific source of root-knot; fire-weed multiplies tomato blight; pepper grass harbors club-root; and so we might continue for a long time to enumerate the diseases of crops that will grow on weeds. Another pernicious effect of weeds is the untidy appearance they present when allowed to grow. When dry they invite fire and are often the road to the destruction of much property.

WATER AND WATERING.

In all vegetable and fruit growing, the question of watering is an important one; it is a necessary factor from the time the seed is planted to the time the crop is harvested. A sufficient amount of water must be applied either naturally or artificially. Where it can be supplied, either by artesian wells or by irrigation, the vegetable grower has a considerable advantage over his neighbors who have not this supply. In dry seasons his crops will not suffer from drouth, and the crop will bring more money in consequence of its shortness elsewhere. Much of our vegetable land can be supplied with water from artesian wells; their usefulness in this respect has already been demonstrated. Another source of water for use in vegetable growing, and one that is not being employed to any considerable extent in the South, is the flowing streams. In many cases there is enough flowing water to supply all or a great portion of the land with water in dry times. Water may be raised to considerable height by the use of a hydraulic ram. One of these machines will run without any attention after it has been put in place and put to running. A single discharge may be quite small, yet when it runs twenty-four hours without stopping a considerable amount of water will have been lifted. The amount of water that one of these machines will raise depends on the height the water is being raised and the amount of water that is flowing in the stream that supplies the water. Under the most favorable conditions a ram will raise two sevenths of the flowing water four feet, if there is a fall of two feet; or it may raise one twentieth the water one hundred and twenty feet above the source if there is a fall of twelve feet. The amount of water raised varies inversely as the height to which it is to be raised. These rams are made in various sizes to suit the conditions; they are made to discharge from one-half to thirty and even more gallons per minute. The cost of the machine varies from $9 to over a $100. Like all other machines it will in time wear out, but its structure is so simple that it rarely gets out of order. The manner of placing the tank or reservoir must be modified to suit the individual fields.

SEED-GROWING.

This is a practice that has not been followed to a decided extent in the South, and yet it is highly commendable. It requires considerable forethought and work to grow the best seed. In some thickly-settled countries of Europe, large estates are devoted entirely to the growing of some special seed, either because of some peculiar natural advantage or because of the tact of its possessor. The Netherlands are peculiarly adapted to bulb-raising, Denmark to raising of cauliflower seed; and thus we might continue until nearly all the countries of Europe had been named. The possibilities in this direction for the South, especially the Gulf region, are exceedingly great; the climatic conditions in many respects are perfect, while labor is efficient and cheap.

HOW TO SELECT PLANTS.

In growing seed, one should never keep a sickly or diseased specimen, because these often transmit a tendency to invite disease in the product of that seed. Only the healthiest and most desirable plants of a variety are good for seed. Some vegetables cannot be raised from home-grown seed; in some cases the seed does not mature, and in others the plants from the home-grown seed are very inferior; a striking example of the latter class is the Bermuda onion. After the finest specimens of the variety have been selected, the plant should be allowed to mature the seed thoroughly before gathering. In propagating plants, there are two directions in which one may select: The first is, to select the most perfect specimens of plants from the standpoint of growth and shape. The second is, to select the finest specimens of fruit regardless of the plant. Neither of these methods are perfect, but one should select the perfect fruits from the most perfect plants. By such selecting, the variety is constantly improved until it finally amounts to enough difference to make a new variety which shall have none of the defects of its ancestors.

It sometimes occurs that a plant appears that is strikingly different from the others in the field. Such plants are often designated "sports"; the seed from these will reproduce these peculiarities, and by selecting the typical specimens from the product of such sports, new varieties may be originated. This method is less profitable and not so certain of a good product.

HOW TO TEST THE VITALITY OF SEED.

As so much depends on having seed that will germinate readily, it is very important to know exactly what to expect in the matter. A very simple method is to sow the seed in a pan that can be kept constantly moist and warm. There is considerable risk connected with this method, and one needs to exercise much care and judgment. The amount of soil in one of these pans will be small, and easily chilled or overheated. A modification of the above is to cover the soil with a cloth, sow the seed on this, cover the seed with another cloth, and put about a half inch of moist sand on this cloth. The advantage in this way is that the seeds can be examined easily, and in case of their rotting, there is no delay in finding it out. The seed may also be tested in a hot-bed or cold frame—using the same precautions as where a pan is used.

Some European countries have seed-control stations under the direction of the governments. These institutions test the vitality of the seed offered for sale and examine them as to purity, thus protecting the buyers from frauds and encouraging the improvement in these directions. Something has been done in that line by the Experiment Station of North Carolina, and it is to be hoped that much more will be accomplished.

The length of time that seeds may be stored without loosing their vitality, depends largely upon the variety and the condition in which they are kept. To keep well, seeds should be well matured and preserved in a dry apartment. Much has been said as to the germinating power of seeds that have been kept for hundreds of years, but these reports lack confirmation by scientific people. Some seeds have been germinated that have been kept dry for thirty and forty years; and recently, there seems to be a creditable report of some seeds retaining their germinating powers for over a hundred years, but in all of these cases this power had been greatly impaired. A few seeds, such as that of cucumbers, retain their vitality under proper conditions for ten years; other seeds lose their vitality during the first year, under the most favorable conditions.

SEED SOWING.

Considerable difficulty is experienced in the matter of seed sowing, especially if the crop is to be sown in the field. Some small seed, as turnips, are very difficult to sow evenly by hand; but, fortunately, this has been overcome in a measure by the invention of a machine to do this work. Even with a machine there is plenty of room for exercise of judgment; seeds of the same variety are not all of the same size, and the average size varies to a considerable extent.

HOW TO TEST A MACHINE.

Before sowing with a machine, it is necessary to know just how it will sow. The marks put on by the manufacturer are only approximately correct, on account of the variation in the size of seed. The machine can be reguaged for the particular seed in hand by running it over a piece of canvas that has been spread down for the occasion. The length of the row on the canvas can be measured and the amount of seed also; this reduces it to a simple computation and the seed can be taken up easily and returned to the bag unharmed. Seed obtained from different sources will be found to vary considerably in size; these seeds of different sizes should be planted separately, and it may be necessary to reguage the machine. It has been found by experiment that there is a wide difference in the value of the different sizes of seed. If radish seed be taken from a single plant and graded into sizes, the largest will germinate and produce a marketable vegetable first, and nearly all the seed produce good radishes; the second size seed will mature radishes next, and so on until the smallest grade is reached, which will produce radishes last and then only inferior roots.

SELECTING VARIETIES.

In this day of specialization, varieties are almost endless; new ones are brought to notice almost daily. Sometimes it seems that the prices paid for these are fabulous, especially when we have first-class vegetables of that kind. It is misdirected economy, however, to buy an inferior variety. The difference of a few dollars at seed time often works a damage of many times that amount at harvest time. Nurserymen and seedsmen prefer to destroy inferior seed or culls of varieties they hold in esteem. This is a commendable practice to apply to all varieties by those who grow seed; inferior seed wastes the time of the person giving attention to it, and damages the reputation of the variety.

QUANTITY OF SEED TO SOW.

The following table gives the amount of seed required for an acre, and also the amount to sow a smaller area. The last column is for the convenience of those who do not wish to grow that especial vegetable for market. A slight acquaintance with the seeds will make us aware at once that these figures can be only approximately correct. Only the leading vegetables are here tabulated; the amounts of others must be sought in the special discussion for that vegetable:

SEED-SOWING.

Name of Plant.	Quantity for One Acre.	Quantity for Smaller Area.
Asparagus	5 pounds	1 oz. to 100 feet, drill.
Beans, bush sorts	1¼ bushels	1 qt. to 150 feet, drill.
" pole	½ bushel	1 qt. to 200 hills.
Beets	10 pounds	1 oz. to 100 feet, drill.
Cabbage	5 ounces	1 oz. to 100 feet, drill.
Cauliflower	5 ounces	1 oz. to 100 feet, drill.
Celery (old culture)	4 ounces	1 oz. to 500 feet, drill.
" (new culture)	32 ounces	1 oz. to 500 feet, drill.
Collards	4 ounces	1 oz. to 100 feet, drill.
Corn (sweet)	8 quarts	1 qt. to 500 hills.
Cucumbers	1¼ pounds	1 oz. to 90 hills.
Egg plant	3 ounces	1 oz. to 500 feet, drill.
Lettuce	3 pounds	1 oz. to 250 feet, drill.
Melon, musk	1¾ pounds	1 oz. to 100 hills.
" water	1½ pounds	1 oz. to 25 hills.
Okra	10 pounds	1 oz. to 50 feet, drill.
Onions	4 pounds	1 oz. to 200 feet, drill.
" sets	8 bushels	1 qt. to 30 feet, drill.
Peas, English	1½ bushels	1 qt. to 150 feet, drill.
" cow	1 bushel	
Pepper	4 ounces	1 oz. to 500 feet, drill.
Potatoes, Irish	10 bushels	
" sweet	(refer to topic)	
Radish	8 pounds	1 oz. to 150 feet, drill.
Salsify	8 pounds	1 oz. to 60 feet, drill.
Spinach	10 pounds	1 oz. to 150 feet, drill.
Squash, summer	2 pounds	1 oz. to 40 hills.
" winter	3 pounds	1 oz. to 10 hills.
Tomato	3 ounces	1 oz. to 500 feet, drill.
Tobacco	2 ounces	1 oz. to bed 6 x 12 feet.
Turnips	1½ pounds	1 oz. to 250 feet, drill.

HOT-BEDS.

This very convenient form of plant-bed is not as generally used in the South as it merits; probably from the fact that many persons do not understand the principles underlying a successful operation of the same.

When any undecomposed manure, leaves or other vegetable matter begins to decay, a certain amount of hea' is given off; if the pile is large and in a compact heap, the amount of heat evolved will be considerable. This is due to the breaking down of plant tissues through the actions of low forms of life, such as bacteria and molds. This breaking down takes place in the presence of moisture; vegetable matter stored in a dry state, will remain undecomposed for an indefinite time. An application of this fact will make it possible for every one who keeps a horse or cow to provide himself with a hot bed.

During the early part of the season the manure may be stored away dry, and kept so, and when the time to fix a hot-bed comes, it may be prepared in a way similar to making a compost heap.

SELECTION OF A LOCATION.

Four points should be borne in mind when one is selecting the place for a hot bed—

First. It must be sheltered from cold winds—that is, it should be in a warm spot; there should be a windbreak of some kind; the bed should be free to the full sun all day; the south side of the barn may be used in some cases.

Second. It must be protected from rains; the drippings of eaves must be carried away and the surface drained so that water will not run under.

Third. Water must be handy, or the needed supply may not be applied.

Fourth. It must be near one's house or near his daily work, so as to require the least possible time to look after it.

CONSTRUCTION.

Glazed sashes are of great value in using a hot-bed successfully, but they are not indispensable. These sashes come set up and glazed in various sizes; probably the most convenient is three by six feet, and can be obtained in the market for about $1.50 apiece. In the Lower South, only a few days occur during the usual winters when the thermometer will remain below freezing if the sun shines. When glazed sashes are not used, some form of cloth will be required. There may be found on the market now a cloth prepared for that purpose; this comes in three grades. The best of these three grades will be found the cheapest in the end. By using a double thickness of the best cloth, we were able to carry egg plants through a freeze of 14° F., and the temperature remained below the freezing point for several days. As egg-plants are among the most tender plants, it will be readily understood that ordinary plants can be carried through easily. During the same freeze, lettuce-plants came through all right under a single thickness of cloth over a cold frame.

The best width for a hot-bed is six feet; at this width, all the cultivating and other attention can be given without entering the frame, and lumber cuts economically to this length. The length of the hot-bed must depend upon the individual desires and preparation. Beds made six feet wide are run east and west, but if it is desirable to run them north and south, the beds should be made twelve feet wide. In such a hotbed, the cloth is fastened to a pole along the middle as a ridge-pole, and allowed to unroll roof-shape on each side. All materials used in their construction may be one inch thick. The back or north sides should be twenty-six inches high, and the south sides ten inches high. When glazed sash are used, a pitch of four inches is sufficient—that is, the front is made ten inches high and the back fourteen. But experience has taught us that this pitch is not sufficient for frames covered with plant-cloth. The sides are nailed to four-inch boards that are driven into the ground six feet apart. The ends of the frame are trimmed to an even slope. At intervals of six feet, three-inch pieces are dove tailed into the front and back, to steady the sides, and to hold the protecting cloth from bagging.

The protecting cloth is sewed into a sheet large enough to cover an entire frame. The seams run crosswise for obvious reasons. The sheet is fastened to the back and then stretched over the frame; and just far enough over the front to press the cloth down tightly, a strip is nailed to serve as a roller for a curtain. By turning at one end, the whole curtain may be raised and fastened at the top; when it is wanted for use, the fastening is loosened and the curtain unrolls itself, at the same time shutting the whole frame up for the night. The wood work and cloth for a frame six feet wide and thirty feet long should not cost more than $2.50.

USING THE MANURE.

When the frame for the hot-bed has been completed, the undecomposed manure is placed in it to the depth of six to ten inches. It is usually necessary to remove some of the earth inside the frame; this can be used to bank it on the outside. As the manure is placed in the frame, it should be thoroughly soaked and tramped down. In two or three days this will begin to heat, and will continue to rise in temperature for eight or ten days, and will often rise high, running considerably over a hundred degrees. If the bed is kept moist, and this can be tested by digging into parts of it, there is no danger of its "burning." This does not mean that there is any danger of it actually generating fire, but the stuff becomes dry and discharges valuable fertilizing quality as gases, and hence is about destroyed. When large quantities of fresh manure are used, the gardeners dump it in piles, and fork it over every day or two to keep it cool enough, and at the end of ten days or two weeks place it in the hot-bed.

After the manure has been placed in the frame, an inch of fresh loam should be spread over it, to arrest any gases that may be escaping. After about ten days of fermenting, the manure has reached its highest temperature, and seed can be sown in the loam without danger. From this time on, the temperature falls gradually, until decomposition is complete.

The only advantage a hot-bed has over a cold-frame is that the decomposing matter gives off heat, and the amount of heat given off will vary with the amount of manure used. If one desires to keep a bed extra warm, the frame may be banked with fresh manure.

PREPARING A COLD-FRAME.

The frame-work and cover are prepared in the same way as for hot-bed. Cold-frames require less fertilizer, and hence are cheaper than hot-beds. The soil in them should be made very fertile by using commercial fertilizer, or, preferably, compost. Make the soil about six inches deep, using about as much well-rotted compost as soil. The fertilizer must be worked in thoroughly, and the frame thus prepared allowed to stand ten days or two weeks, all the time keeping it thoroughly moistened. A cold frame is as valuable in the summer as in the winter. In the summer, the cloth is raised to allow air to pass under, thus protecting small plants from the scorching sun. In the management of a cold-frame, and of a hot-bed, plenty of water is indispensable, and it must be applied in liberal quantities daily.

PREPARATION OF A PLANT-BED.

Plant-beds are very largely employed in the South for raising seedlings, especially tobacco. A cold-frame will serve every purpose of a plant-bed for raising seedlings, and has many advantages. Seedlings, after growing to a size that are easily handled, are often planted in a bed for further maturing; this is especially so when large quantities of tomato, cabbage or celery plants are wanted. The advantage of having these plants in as small a space as practicable is apparent to all. The plant-bed must be very fertile, and have plenty of water to be used in case of need. The ground should be raked carefully, the fertilizer applied, and the bed spaded or plowed and then raked again. The bed should lie a week or ten days to allow the fertilizer to be incorporated, when the plants may be set out. Plants should not be allowed to become checked in their growth at any time. It does plants good to be transferred several times, and with some vegetables such transplanting is profitable; but, for plants to come to a standstill for want of water or fertilizer, works a detriment that is strikingly noticeable in the crop. Hence, in the transplantings, great care should be taken as to moisture, temperature and soil, so that growth may not be checked.

PREPARATION OF THE LAND.

To make vegetable growing a success, it is necessary to select the proper kind of land. Nearly all vegetables like a sandy loam or some other rather light soil, that is at the same time well drained and yet not thirsty.

LAND WELL DRAINED.

It frequently occurs that the very best vegetable land is soggy and sour in its original state. When we find a piece of land that is excellent in all other respects, but needs to be drained, the problem that then concerns us is, How shall this be effected? When there is plenty of fall to the land, this may be accomplished in one of two ways—either by surface drainage or by underground drainage. The latter method is the preferable one and the cheaper one in the end, though the more expensive in the beginning.

The method of surface drainage has the advantage of being cheap and easily accomplished, though it takes some time and attention to keep it in good running order. The method is simple. All that is necessary is to make a ditch from one to three feet deep and keep this open so the water will run off.

The advantage of draining has been demonstrated repeatedly in this country and in Europe. Plants on tile drained land, and to a greater or less degree on land with open ditch, will do better during a rainy season, and, what seems rather contradictory, they will give a larger yield in dry years. Crops are also earlier on drained fields. In a clay country, land that is well drained naturally will be benefitted by a well-planned system of tile drains. Where land that is well drained naturally can be obtained, this is preferred, of course, as it does away with the initial expense of draining; but, on the other hand, it should be remembered that the land producing the largest and most profitable crop is drained land.

CLEAR THE LAND.

In making a beginning in vegetable growing, it is best to start aright. The greater portion of our unimproved land has to be cleared, and this should be done thoroughly; every stalk, stick or chunk should be removed from the field. It is a waste of time and money to go into vegetable growing as a temporary vocation; it is as deserving and demanding of constant and careful attention as any other branch of horticulture. So if you can clear ten acres only half way, why, you had better clear five acres all the way. It has been seen repeatedly that a small piece of land well taken care of brought a greater return than double the amount cared for poorly. The familiar adage, "What is worth doing is worth doing well," has full force in vegetable growing.

SHALL WE PLOW DEEP?

If we have a light, sandy soil, deep plowing may prove detrimental to a field that is to be planted immediately, but some time during the year it should be stirred deeply and well. The subsoil is often so hard that the roots of the crop cannot enter, and so have to stay near the surface and be at the mercy of any short drought that may occur; whereas, if the soil were twice as deep, it could stand a much longer drouth. Many subsoils do not allow the water to soak through them; other subsoils let the surplus water through slowly. In either case, the mechanical condition of the soil would be improved by an occasional deep plowing. Besides giving the roots a greater feeding space, the tilling of the soil acts as a kind of a regulator; it makes soggy land drier and dry land to conserve the moisture in it. A cultivated soil can hold more water without being soggy than one that is not tilled; in a sudden shower a plowed field will retain all the water and give the roots of plants a chance to absorb the fertilizer before it is carried off. Much of our sandy land allows the fertilizer to be leached out by the rains and retains not even a trace in the soluble form; but if this water were retained in the soil the fertilizer would be retained also. The amount of water a soil can retain depends upon the constituent particles of that soil.

NUMBER OF PLANTS PER ACRE.

The following table gives the number of plants per acre when they are set at given distances. If we desire to find the number of plants required to set an acre at distances not given in the table below, this can be done by a slight amount of forethought. The number of plants for one inch asunder in the row are given. If then, plants are set two inches apart, the field will require just half as many; if three inches, just one-third as many as when one inch apart; and if seven inches apart, just one-seventh the number.

Distance between the rows.		Distance between plants in the row.		Number of plants required to the acre.	Distance between the rows.		Distance between plants in the row.		Number of plants required to the acre.
Ft.	In.	Ft.	In.		Ft.	In.	Ft.	In.	
0	6	0	6	174,240	3	0	1	0	14,520
0	7	0	7	128,013	3	0	1	6	9,680
0	8	0	8	98,010	3	0	2	0	7,260
1	0	0	1	522,720	3	0	2	6	5,808
1	0	0	6	87,120	3	0	3	0	4,840
1	0	1	0	43,560	4	0	0	6	21,780
1	6	0	1	348,480	4	0	0	9	14,520
1	6	0	6	58,080	4	0	1	0	10,890
1	6	1	0	29,040	4	0	1	6	7,260
1	6	1	6	19,360	4	0	2	0	5,445
2	0	0	3	87,120	4	0	2	6	4,356
2	0	0	6	43,560	4	0	3	0	3,630
2	0	1	0	21,780	4	0	3	6	3,111
2	0	1	6	14,520	4	0	4	0	2,722
2	0	2	0	10,890	5	0	5	0	1,742
3	0	0	6	29,066	6	0	5	0	1,452
3	0	0	9	19,360	6	0	6	0	1,210

TRANSPLANTING.

Under this head we will consider also the transplanting of plants from one bed to another. Soon after plants that have been sown in a seed-bed begin to show the second or third leaf, they will need to be shifted and set out thinner, or they will grow spindly and leggy. Then, also, their root system will be developed very poorly, and after transplanting they will either have to change their entire make up as a plant or die; either one of the two is expensive, as it loses time for the vegetable-grower. Some plants, as cabbage and cauliflower, will do well with one shifting; others, as tomatoes and egg-plants, will do the better for having been shifted two or three times. A very good way is to have a hot-bed to grow the plants from the seed, then shift them to a cold-frame; this will have to be many times larger than the hot-bed to hold the same plants. It will not take long for the plants to fill the space allowed them (for distance and other special points refer to the special crops); then another transfer will have to be made either to a cold-frame or to a plant-bed, depending on the variety and time of the year. As mentioned before, the soil in this should contain much undecomposed vegetable matter. If this precaution be taken, it will not be necessary to wait for a rain or to use water in transplanting. If paper pots (which can be bought for $2 or $3 per thousand) are used, the plant can be transplanted from the plant-bed quickly and without shock to the plant at all.

In fertilizing the land preparatory to transplanting, the material should be worked in and mixed with the soil thoroughly. It does not matter how small a particle of fertilizer may be in the soil, the plants will find it. The thorough distribution is very necessary. Plants cannot take in such substances in a wholesale style; while some kinds of fertilizer do not kill a plant when used in big lumps, a very large proportion of such doses is not available, or only so after considerable time. We rarely use too much fertilizer, but use it indiscretely.

The best time to transplant is just before a rain; but where there are ten or twenty acres to be planted, the work must go ahead when the proper time comes, whether there is a rain at hand or not. It is certainly no easy task to put out and water an acre of tomatoes or half an acre of cabbage in a day.

Considerable of this hard work may be avoided by using a transplanter. Many machines have been constructed and put on the market to do this work. Some are operated by hand, allowing a person to stand in a partially erect position. They do the work more or less efficiently, but for the lack of perfection, none have come into general use. There are also machines that are drawn by horses, but the plants must be put in place by hand. Some of these machines do excellent work, and would be used generally, but the prices of the machines are so high that many cannot buy them, and some who can buy them, dislike to pay more for a machine than it is worth. The greatest advantage in the machine drawn by horses is, that a regulated quantity of water is emptied wherever a plant is to be placed. To use one of these machines, the land must be free from *debris*. Stumps and trees are also in the way. The amount that can be planted in a day depends upon the crop and the condition of the land. It is said that six or seven acres of tomatoes can be planted in a day.

MARKETING.

It is not difficult to find persons who have labored diligently to produce a good crop, and then put it on the market in a slovenly manner. Fancy prices are paid for fancy fruits and vegetables, but it is necessary to have the package fancy from the beginning to end; any one point in the whole series will work a decided damage to it all. It requires more brains to produce a fine article, hence the supply is limited. It is more profitable to produce the best of everything, so the mere statement at this place is sufficient. If we wish to succeed in any line of business, we must offer for sale the article that is wanted, and as long as there is monopoly of that article, the price is considerably above the cost of production. Often, the mere style of label on a package makes a difference of 10 per cent. in the selling price. The street venders in our large cities learn to know human nature well; they will buy good vegetables and fruits that have been shipped in poor packages, and take the time and trouble to repack them, and find it a profitable employment. Florida Lecoute pears shipped in old barrels, are packed and wrapped to make California Bartletts. We must emphasize the matter of doing the very best with the best material at hand. If a crop is all culls, nine times out of ten it will not pay to market it at all.

THE PACKING-HOUSE.

To put vegetables on the market in first class style requires certain equipments. One of the indispensables is a good packing-house. When vegetables and fruit are ready for the market, they must be sent out; they cannot wait. One cannot stop to plan a packing-house after the crop begins to ripen nor is this the time to build one.

A good packing-house is airy and roomy, and so constructed that all parts can be kept clean. It has been demonstrated several times that vegetables have contracted disease in the packing-house, and arrived in the market in an unsalable condition. In several cases this led to an annoying controversy, and one in which both parties, being entirely sincere, were severe losers—the buyers in losing a very desirable trade and the vegetable-growers in having to pay for shipping a quantity of worthless vegetables. We cannot say that this was because of carelessness on the part of the vegetable-grower, but rather because of a lack of knowledge on the subject. Diseased vegetables should not be brought into the packing-house, nor should they be left in the field; this is a subject, however, that deserves special attention, and should be discussed at length under the subject of plant diseases.

The location of a packing-house must be decided by each individual, as the points to be taken into consideration are of an individual character. Where it is possible to place it so the vegetables can be loaded directly on to the car, this will compensate for considerable disadvantage in other ways, as it saves one handling of full crates. After this, the question as to whether it shall be in the field or near one's dwelling has to be disposed of; we must then examine the ground. In the planning of a house a few general principles may be given that will cover all kinds of vegetables; there must be more or less variation in detail to suit the kind of vegetable to be packed. The product should enter on one side and be taken out on another. The driveway to the entrance should be high enough so the vegetables do not have to be lifted to the floor.

The arrangement should be such that the crop does not have to be lifted at each successive handling. It is easier to lift a crate of vegetables from a bench than it is to place it on the bench. Most laborers will do more efficient work when not tired than after they become tired. A tired laborer works to the detriment of the grower whether the pay is "by the box" or by the day. The packing season is a busy one, and laborers are often hard to obtain; if, then, four laborers can do the work of five, there will be that much more for profit or margin for investment.

The practice of packing poor products in the centre of the crate cannot be too strongly condemned, and the persons who make a practice of this usually reap the reward. Too often, however, they at the same time do a great injury to their neighbor. "Honesty is the best policy."

HOW TO MAKE A CRATE.

The material for making crates is supplied at such reasonable figures that it does not pay a vegetable-grower to work up his own lumber. The ordinary vegetable crates are made of rough lumber, but some of the tomato crates, which are used for the fancy articles, are very tastefully made of dressed lumber. A bushel crate is eight inches by fourteen inches by two feet. These usually have a partition in the middle, but for some vegetables, as English peas or string beans, this is not necessary, but possibly profitable. These pieces may be obtained already cut to size, consequently all that is left for the vegetable-grower to do is to nail them together. The ends are eight by fourteen inches, and have the corners cut off so as to make it eight-sided. The sides are made of quarter inch material, three inches wide.

A labor saving device may be made by nailing some cleats on the floor or work-bench to hold the ends and middle in place while one of the sides is being nailed. Fasten two cleats just far enough apart so a crate-end will be held up sideway between them; then just two feet from the outer edge of this side nail down two more cleats that will hold up another end in a similar way. The outer sides of these ends should be just two feet apart. Midway between these fasten two more cleats—these are to hold the partition of the crate. The side-slats can now be nailed to the ends and partition very easily. This will give sufficient support to the ends and partition of the box, that it may be turned over and the other side nailed on. A slat nailed on to each corner, which has been sawed off and one of the eight-inch sides nailed up, and the crate will be ready to receive vegetables.

A barrel crate, or one that will hold about a hundred pounds of cabbage, may be made in a similar way. The dimensions of such a crate are twelve inches by eighteen inches by three feet. The slats for such crates must be broader and thicker.

MUSHROOMS.

Mushrooms do not belong to the flowering plants, and are probably on this account not treated in many books on vegetable growing; while it may not be altogether logical to treat them here, it will be noticed upon observation that the markets class them with vegetables, and any one who has a good knowledge of vegetable growing can become a mushroom grower. The underlying principles are not so different as the unitiated imagine. Under this head are classed many different species of plants belonging to a number of genera. The spawn or "seed" is obtained from wild specimens frequently, but that sent out by seed houses is grown under cultivation. Many of the wild species may be used as they occur in their native habitat, but it is not well for one not familiar with the edible ones to make use of such without being advised by those who are familar with the edible ones. While the number of poisonous ones are much smaller than is generally believed, and their poisonous character much less dangerous than many persons give credit for, it is good sense to permit those famiilar with the plants to do the choosing. If one uses spawn sent out by the seed houses and raises a crop from this no trouble need be anticipated, or if those offered for sale are used there is no danger.

The food value of these esculents is not usually recognized in this country, but they are rather looked upon as tid-bits. They are especially rich in protein, a food element often deficient in our diet. *Morchella esculenta* contains thirty-five per cent. of it; *Boletus edulus* twenty-two per cent. ; while bread contains only eight per cent. France exports millions of dollars worth annually, while our country does not supply her wants.

PREPARATION OF THE BED.

Fresh manure of various kinds will be found best in preparing a mushroom bed. The best success is obtained by using fresh manure of horses fed on grain; the manure of horses fed exclusively on hay is not as good—in fact, quite poor. When any considerable amount of manure has been collected, it should be mixed thoroughly to make it as even as possible and then piled. In this state it may be allowed to heat and decompose partially. If a bed can be constructed in a dark place, as under buildings, it will obviate the necessity of preparing a cover; otherwise, it will be necessary to provide one to shut out the light (see Fig. 1). In some forcing houses beds are placed under the benches. Old sheds also may be utilized. After the manure has passed through its first heating it may be placed in the bed, which may be made similar to a hotbed; the manure being tramped in a foot to two feet' thick, and should be kept moist constantly but never soaked.

Near the city of Paris, France, are many underground quarries to supply building stone to the metropolis; at intervals piers are left to support the mass above. When portions of these quarries are abandoned and left as empty rooms, they are claimed by mushroom growers to plant gardens. While the surface of the land may be growing wheat, beneath it in the interior of the earth is a crop of mushroom. From these underground gardens an average of 300 pounds of mushrooms are brought up daily.

Soon after filling a bed the temperature rises, often reaching 100° F. During this time it must be watched closely that it does not become dry and "burn out." In a few days the temperature will return to 90° F., and then fall gradually until it reaches the temperature of the surrounding soil. When a bed reaches the temperature of 90° F. the spawn may be put in, but some mushroom growers prefer to wait until 70° F. is reached. If one waits until this temperature has been reached there will be less danger of losing the spawn. The temperature of the bed should not be allowed to fall below 55° F. For those who are not familiar with this work it will be well to have a hole in the bed at intervals of three or four feet to enable one to insert a thermometer for ascertaining the temperature.

Fig. 1.
Figure 1 represents a mushroom bed on a bench similar to those used in forcing houses.

The spawn is usually obtained in bricks. A cubic inch of spawn is enough for about eighty square inches of bed. The bricks are broken into pieces of about a cubic inch, and then placed an inch or so under the surface of the bed; if the bed is quite warm, the spawn is put nearer the surface; if quite cool, it may be placed even deeper. Under favorable conditions one will have some mushrooms coming in for use in two months from the time of spawning.

ASPARAGUS.

This vegetable is not grown very extensively in the South. While there are several reports of success we have more reports of failures. These reports of failures would not have been recorded in so many instances if the proper attention had been given to fertilization and cultivation. In the States where it is grown for the New York markets it is not uncommon to spend from $300 to $600 per acre for fertilizer. Manure from the large cities is employed to a considerable extent, but chemical fertilizer may be employed with profit.

Mr. F. Brill, in his Farm Gardening and Seed Growing, says: "As a rule, asparagus succeeds best near the sea coast, though it can be (and is) profitably grown far inland, upon most any soil, by proper cultivation and careful attention, and, in fact, this is a very essential point and the great secret of success in any locality." The point emphazied by Mr. Brill is the one overlooked by most growers. Somehow the idea has become current that asparagus will do well under any treatment, and no attention is required except to gather the crop. In selecting the field it should be moist and yet not wet; a water-soaked piece will not grow this crop. While it wants an abundance of moisture it must not be sour. Land that has been drained often makes the best plots.

PREPARATION OF THE PLOT.

Deep plowing, to loosen up the subsoil, is the first act after the plot has been drained. Among the best growers the opinion is held that it is difficult to make the land too rich or have it too well prepared. The roots penetrate the soil deeply and to a great extent;

it is what gardeners term a gross feeder. The fertilizer usually employed contains a great deal of organic matter, such as compost and rakings from yards; this is mixed thoroughly with the soil and is often applied before the plants are set out. After they have started a top dressing of potash and phosphoric acid is given. When the plantation is made considerable distance from the sea coast it is customary to give a heavy application of salt; this may be applied without injury at the rate of two pounds per square yard.

PLANTING.

The quickest and surest way to make a beginning in asparagus-growing is to buy several hundred or a thousand roots from a seedsman. These are not expensive, and will make a fair test as to whether it will be desirable or not to go into growing it as a business.

Lay off rows three feet apart and set the plants a foot to eighteen inches apart in the row. During the first year the field should be well worked and no weeds allowed to get a start. The second year less cultivation will do.

FIG. 2.

Figure 2 is a cut of an asparagus buncher that may be obtained on the market for a small price. By referring to this one it will be easily understood how to construct one at home.

Plants one, two and three years old may be obtained in the market. The two-year-old plants will be found to be the best, and are usually a little higher priced than the others.

CUTTING.

While plants will be found to give a few stems one year from transplanting, it is better practice to let them grow up and cut only sparingly, even the second year. In gathering, care should be taken to cut all the thin, spindly stems and leave a few strong shoots to form a leaf system for the plant. In cutting, a little of the soil is removed and the asparagus knife is then pushed down carefully so as not to injure any of the stems that are just beginning to push up. A slight twist of the knife will separate the stem from the root.

BUNCHING AND CRATING.

The stems are usually cut when they are about six inches above the grouna, and then cutting these three or four inches below the ground makes them nine or ten inches long. The stems are laid into some kind of a contrivance, either home made or bought, that will keep them straight and keep the tips even (see Fig. 2). A simple buncher is made by using a board 8 by 12 inches; nail to the end of this a thin board, 8 by 8 inches; nail on to the 8 by 12 piece three or four U shaped iron straps, so they will be parallel to the 8 by 8 inch board, and that when the asparagus is laid into these the heads will butt against the board. This 8 by 8 inch board will keep the heads even and the U-shaped straps make the bunch round. Strings of raffia or soft cord are laid across the buncher, and when enough of the vegetable to make a bunch has been added the whole is tied tightly, as shown in the illustration (Fig. 3). Then with a sharp knife cut the butts square and the work is done. A handier buncher may be obtained from dealers in garden implements at a small cost. Such a buncher will be found profitable where much asparagus is to be prepared for market (see Fig. 2).

FIG. 3.

MARKETING.

A carrier for shipping to a distant market must be either a half crate or one divided so as to hold only one tier of bunches in a compartment. Place some soft moist material, as moss or grass, in the bottom and set the bunches upright on this; cover with the same soft material and put a cover over the tier. Another tier may be put above in the same manner as described for the first. These crates must be sent to the market right side up. Care must also be taken not to bruise or otherwise mutilate the stems, as this is liable to induce them to rot in transit.

BLANCHING.

Often asparagus is not cultivated, but this may be done with profit. It too often happens that it is allowed to go to seed. This falling between the rows obliterates them, besides crowding the plants, which makes the stalks come up slender and too small for market. If all seed stalks are cut off before the berries are half grown, this difficulty will be obviated. To blanch the product, a furrow is thrown upon the row from each side and raked level. By so doing the plants are buried several inches deeper than they grew. The light being excluded from the growing shoot, no chlorophyll forms until the tip bursts through the ground, when the cutting should be done. After the winter frosts have killed the plants to the ground, the tops may be removed and composted and the bed raked, to be ready for early spring cutting. While our markets do not call for blanched asparagus, the blanched article will sell first when both are on the same market and offered for the same price, indicating that there is a decided preference for the blanched article.

RAISING PLANTS.

During summer certain of the stalks produce flowers, and later, seed; this is in the form of small berries about the size of a pea. When the berries are ripe they turn a bright red, and in a short time are liable to fall from the plant. When the seed is desired, it will be necessary to collect the plants containing the seed for storing and preserving. As stated before, if one does not want to save the seed, all plants bearing flowers or green seed should be cut off to keep the bed from being crowded by seedlings that would spring up from these seeds if allowed to fall. Another way of getting the seed is to go into the field and strip off the ripe seed by hand. If the plants are cut to obtain the seed, they should be dried, when the seed may be beaten off on a cloth. The seed is so common that there is no sale for it.

Prepare a rich piece of land by plowing deeply, and lay off rows about twenty inches apart; drop the seed about an inch apart in a drill and cover an inch deep. When the plants are four or five inches high, thin out to one in four or five inches. If the plants are to remain two years in the seed drills, thin out to six inches apart. In this case drop the seed farther apart. It is quite certain that it is more profitable to grow the plants to two years old before setting out to the field.

CANNING.

Much of the asparagus used in the South has been canned. The operation is similar to that for other vegetables and fruit.

VARIETIES.

Giant Brunswick is one of the best for the South; Palmetto is also very productive and a general favorite. The variation in the different varieties is probably less than in most vegetables. The same variety under different treatment often varies more than different varieties under similar treatment.

FERTILIZER FORMULA.

Nitrogen .... 4 per cent.
Potash... ....5 "
Available phosphoric acid ......7 "

Use 1,500 pounds of the above formula per acre. When possible, apply twenty to forty tons of vegetable material, such as partially rotted rakings or barn-yard manure. Where such vegetable matter is procurable, the quantity of nitrogen may be decreased proportionately. If manure is procurable, allowance should be made for the fertilizer elements contained therein.

An application of salt is usually considered necessary. If kainit is used as a source of potash, we should remember that it contains 30 to 35 per cent. of salt.

The following table will give the amounts of different fertilizer material necessary to give the desired quantity of each element:

Element.   *Pounds of different material for one acre.*

Nitrogen .. ..
- 800 to 1,000 lbs. cotton-seed meal; or
- 350 to 400 lbs. nitrate of soda; or
- 275 to 300 lbs sulphate of ammonia; or
- 400 to 600 lbs. dried blood.

Potash............ ......
- 300 to 500 lbs. kainit; or
- 150 lbs. muriate of potash; or
- 150 lbs. sulphate of potash; or
- 250 to 300 lbs. sulphate of potash.

Phosphoric acid..
- 750 to 1,000 lbs. acid phosphate; or
- 600 to 800 lbs. dissolved bone.

RHUBARB.

This vegetable has not been planted largely in the Gulf region. There seems to be no natural obstacle to its being produced here, and it is doubtless due to the fact that vegetable growing for distant markets is a new industry. This, among others, suffers severely from poor transportation.

A dark sandy loam is a favorable soil; it may even tend to be gravelly, but must not be dry. A well drained clay soil is also good, and preferred by some rhubarb growers. A light soil is liable to allow the plant to produce large roots at the expense of the "stalks," but when the gardener is aware of this, it can be overcome by proper cultivation, or the plants may be taken up and the roots divided.

Whatever kind of land is used, plenty of fertilizer will be required; often fifty to a hundred loads per acre are used on rich vegetable land. Well-rotted muck that has been worked into the soil deeply will be found a fair substitute for manure, but we must not forget to supply the needed potash and phosphoric acid.

PLANTING.

Seed may be obtained from seedsmen and the plants grown this way will require about three years to obtain a crop. It should be remembered, however, that a field will bear for ten years or more under proper treatment. Sow the seed in drills eighteen inches or two feet apart; thin the plants to six inches in the row. The seed may be sown any time in the spring after danger from frost is past; as it is slow to germinate, watering may be found necessary. It should be sown as early as convenient, so as to have as large a leaf system as possible for the summer's heat. As the plants are expensive, it will be well to grow them as soon as one is assured that the proper land and facilities are at hand.

To get a quick start plants should be obtained from a seedsman. Work the manure in as deeply as possible with a team, and be sure that the fertilizer has been worked in well. Lay the land off in rows from four to six feet apart, and set the plants from three to four feet apart in the row, according to the variety of plants and strength of the soil.

It will be two years from the time of setting out to the time that a crop may be expected; during this time the field may be planted to other vegetables, but an additional amount of fertilizer should be supplied. After the by-crop has been removed the plants should be mulched to keep the soil from drying out. It is not a good plan to collect any stalks that may be marketable before the second year.

VARIETIES.

There are several varieties offered on the markets, but we will be safe in planting Linnaeus or Victoria. Mammoth is good, but liable to be woody on poor soil.

FERTILIZER FORMULA.

Nitrogen .... 3 per cent.
Potash .... 7 per cent.
Phosphoric acid .... 8 per cent.

Use 1500 to 2000 pounds of the above fertilizer. Humus is a much needed ingredient in the rhubarb soil; where this cannot be supplied in the form of manure, we should get leaf mold or muck.

The following amounts of fertilizer will give the desired quantity of each essential element:

RHUBARB.

Element.	Pounds of different material for one acre.
Nitrogen............	600 to 800 lbs. cotton-seed meal; or 450 to 600 lbs. dried blood; or 300 to 400 lbs. nitrate of soda; or 200 to 250 lbs. sulphate of ammonia.
Potash............	1200 to 1500 lbs. kainit; or 200 to 250 lbs. muriate of potash; or 200 to 250 lbs. sulphate of potash; or 350 to 450 lbs. sulphate of potash, and sulphate of magnesia.
Phosphoric acid.	900 to 1200 lbs. acid phosphate; or 650 to 900 lbs. dissolved bone.

CULTIVATION.

This, above all other plants, can stand deep and thorough cultivation. In the fall, after the plants have ceased to grow, the ground may be thrown up onto the row by a stirring plow, and this raked or harrowed down again. Usually it is a good thing to cut the roots and check the early feeding. After the field has come into bearing, no other crops should be planted in the field, and the cultivation be simply for the rhubarb. The ground must be cultivated in the spring, but after the pulling season is over, the field will usually take care of itself. The large green leaves shade the ground and prevent other plants from growing, though here and there weeds may spring up; these may be pulled or cut.

MARKETING.

When the field begins to bear, which was stated above to be when the plants are three years old. The earliest leaves are pulled when the stalks are about eight inches long. At this size they are quite tender, and care must be exercised not to injure them in pulling. Later in the season the stalks are allowed to grow longer before pulling, but the earlier ones are the higher priced.

The pullers gather the leaves until they have an armful, when it is laid down beside the road. After a portion of the field has been pulled, a wagon is driven along, and the armsful are placed on this and hauled to the bunching shed. The blades are then cut off and the stalks tied into bunches (see Fig. 4). Some of the varieties are so brittle that it is necessary to let them wilt a short time before tying. The size of the bunch must be such as will suit the market, and this can be learned only by experience.

This vegetable is shipped in ventilated crates or barrels, and as the product is removed from the package before the consumer buys it, there is very little choice in the kind of package. Forced rhubarb is usually tied up in bunches containing six large stalks, which sell for a dollar a bunch; as soon as the outdoor article comes into market the price declines rapidly. Besides being used as a vegetable, it is employed in making wine; for this purpose it has sold for $15.00 a ton.

Fig. 4.

Figure 4 represents stalks of rhubarb ready for crating. This figure represents the stalks cut at the proper length.

FORCING.

The lucrative price paid for fresh rhubarb in the winter has induced many nurserymen to force this vegetable. In the fall, after the frost has fallen, the roots are taken up with as little mutilation as possible and transferred to a hot-bed or greenhouse. If the sale is to be made in early winter the heat is applied at once, but if for later winter market the roots are kept in a dormant state until the proper time has arrived.

The Gulf region will not have to use heat to have early rhubarb. If it is profitable and desirable to force it, the product will stand the cost of transportation.

LETTUCE.

With the increased facility in transportation, the Lower South is beginning to produce lettuce for extentensive Northern markets. The southern portion of Florida, and a strip along the entire Gulf, can grow this vegetable without protection, but further north it will be necessary to have at least protecting cloth or hot-bed sashes to break the cold of some of the severest weather. It can stand a temperature of 20° F. without damage, while some varieties are not killed even at 15° F. Such low temperatures may not kill the plants, but they retard their development; this does not prevent their forming heads, however.

PLANT-BED.

In preparing a cold frame or hot-bed for this vegetable, we should select coarse loam and mix with this plenty of vegetable matter, so as to put lots of humus into the soil. The drainage must be so any surplus water will draw off rapidly.

Sow the seed in shallow drills about three inches apart, and cover lightly. Cover the bed so as to protect it from the sun or too rapid drying. It is a good plan to sprinkle the bed every morning. As soon as the seedlings are up strong, and before the leaves begin to form, the largest are picked out with the point of a knife or a similar tool. These seedlings are then set out in rows four inches apart and put the plants an inch apart in the row.

Only first-class plants should be selected, and the inferior ones destroyed. As soon as the plants are set out, they should be sprinkled thoroughly, and they will grow off without a perceptible check. Before the plants begin to touch in the row, they should be transplanted again; this time placed in checks four by four inches. At this time the largest should be chosen again and the inferior ones destroyed. In a few weeks from this transplanting, the plants will be ready to go to the field. If they are to remain in a cold frame, plant them in checks twelve by twelve inches, or sixteen by sixteen inches, according to the variety. If they are to be planted in the field, make the rows eighteen to twenty-four inches apart and set the plants fourteen inches in the row. The last transplanting should be made before the heads begin to form.

PREPARING THE FIELD.

All rubbish should be removed from the land before the field is plowed; debris of any sort is not only annoying, but also very liable to interfere in cultivating and liable to cause considerable loss.

The soil should be a friable loam, with very little silt or fine sand present. It should be rich, but need not be deep. All plowing and preparation may be shallow.

A handy way to plant in the field is to lay the rows off at proper distances, and then make checks along the row. Then drop a plant at each check, and afterwards come along with a dibber and press the roots into the ground, or the forefinger may be used for this purpose. Press the soil firmly about the plants, and water thoroughly.

CULTIVATION.

If the weather is dry, frequent shallow plowings should be given; it is usually necessary to finish up by hand, but as much work as possible ought to be done by horse-power. During a wet season, the cultivating should be deep and thorough, so as to allow the surplus water to drain off rapidly. It is not sufficient to keep the weeds down, but the soil must be loose and friable all the time.

FERTILIZER FORMULA.

Available phosphoric acid...... 9 per cent.
Potash............................ 12 per cent.
Nitrogen .... 5 per cent.

Use 800 to 1,000 pounds per acre of the above formula. If land is rich in nitrogenous matter, the amount of nitrogen may be cut down to suit the land. In a cold frame or hot-bed, use a pound for every twelve square feet.

The following amounts of materials will give the quantity of each element called for in the formula:

Element.	Pounds of different materials for one acre.
Phosphoric acid.	600 to 1,200 lbs. acid phosphate; or 500 to 1,000 lbs. dissolved bone
Potash............	900 to 1,500 lbs. kainit; or 200 to 250 lbs. muriate of potash; or 200 to 250 lbs. sulphate of potash; or 400 to 500 lbs. sulphate of potash, and sulphate of magnesia.
Nitrogen	600 to 1,200 lbs. cotton-seed meal; or 250 to 500 lbs. muriate of soda; or 200 to 400 lbs. sulphate of ammonia.

FIGURE 5.
Figure 5 represents a lettuce head of the solid varieties ready to ship.

VARIETIES.

The best all-round lettuce is the Grand Rapids.

Blond Blockhead and Black-seeded Simpson are each good head lettuce. (See Figure 5.) There are many other varieties that are claiming attention, but the above will be found reliable.

MARKETING.

The solid head varieties do not remain in a marketable condition as long as the Grand Rapids and those of its type; so if the solid varieties are planted, they will have to be sent forward to the markets when matured. As a whole, the Eastern markets are partial to head lettuce, while the Western markets are more inclined toward loose heads. For local markets, lettuce may be bleached; any simple contrivance that will shut out the sun will do this.

For shipping, the crop must be cut when it is dry. Pack in a barrel or open crate. The heads should be packed in firmly but do not crush the leaves. The packing must be so firm that the material in the crate cannot shake.

RAISING SEED.

For this purpose the plants should be selected just as for market crop. When the plants are mature, all individuals that are not typical should be removed from the field. If any plant contract a disease, it should be removed also.

About six weeks after marketing time, the plants will have sent up a seed stalk. Place a stake in the ground firmly beside each plant and tie the plant to the stake. This will save many plants from being blown over.

The ripening of the seed will be indicated by the feathery pappus on the individual heads. As soon as a goodly number of heads are ripe, the whole plant may be cut off and bunched to be hung for drying in the packing-house. As soon as dry, the seed should be threshed, as it is very easily blown away. Clean out all chaff and light seed and pack away from mice and roaches.

ENDIVE.

This plant is used either as greens or in making salads, but is not demanded in markets of the South. While it is raised to a considerable extent in some places North, it receives greater attention in Europe.

A quick loam is required to make a good crop, but, like spinach, it is a surface-feeder. The land should be thoroughly prepared and the fertilizer evenly distributed.

Make the rows about two feet apart and sow the seed thickly, and thin out later to about nine inches in the row. Sow the seed in September or October.

FIG. 6.
Endive plant ready to cut for market.

About the first of January or February, the crop will be ready to bleach; this is done by tying the outer leaves up over the inner until the green has disappeared. It depends much upon the condition of the weather as to the length of time that will be required in bleaching; if the plants are growing rapidly and the weather is warm, only half as much time will be required as when the weather is cold and plants not growing. Transplanted endive has not yielded as well as when not transplanted, so it is preferable not to transplant, but to sow an abundance of seed and then thin out.

The marketing is like that of spinach.

There are two classes of varieties—the yellow and the green; the yellow is probably the more attractive, but there is little choice.

FERTILIZER FORMULA.

Nitrogen................................ 5 per cent.
Potash................................. 6 per cent.
Available phosphoric acid ..... 6 per cent.

Use 800 to 1,200 pounds of the above formula per acre. If the nitrogen is in the form of vegetable matter, it should be thoroughly decomposed; if in the form of mineral matter, it had better be applied at different times. Apply the fertilizer in the drill.

The following table gives the amounts of different fertilizers required to give the desired quantity of each element:

Element.	Pounds of different material for one acre.
Nitrogen	500 to 750 lbs. cotton-seed meal; or 500 to 600 lbs. dried blood; or 250 to 375 lbs. nitrate of soda; or 200 to 300 lbs. sulphate of ammonia.
Potash	600 to 900 lbs. kainit; or 150 to 225 lbs. muriate of potash; or 150 to 225 lbs. sulphate of potash; or 250 to 375 lbs. sulphate of potash and sulphate of magnesia.
Phosphoric acid	400 to 600 lbs. acid phosphate; or 350 to 500 lbs. dissolved bone.

CHICORY.

This is used very largely in the kitchens of the Netherlands and to some extent in England. The demand that exists for it in this country is not sufficient to call it a market. There are several varieties that are known by different names. Coffee chicory is grown for the roots, which are dried and then used as a substitute for coffee by some of the poorer people of the Netherlands and England. Other varieties are cultivated for their leaves and leaf stalks.

The usual garden soil will be found sufficiently rich for this plant, and will need very little care in the way of preparation. Prepare the rows in a way very similar to that for parsnips and other root crops. Sow in early spring for late spring or summer crop. By sowing in February, it will be fit to use in April or May. Less time will be required for the late summer crop to mature.

The cultivation is very simple, merely enough to keep the weeds down, and the ground somewhat loose. Deep cultivation will be found good. A week or ten days before the leaves are wanted for use, some soil should be worked up to the plant to bleach the stalks and leaves. As soon as these are well bleached, they may be taken to the kitchen and prepared as other vegetables. For winter chicory, the seed should be sown during August or September. It will be necessary to protect it during the summer rains, and also from the hot fall sun. As soon as cold weather comes, the soil may be banked up around it to bleach the leaves, or the leaves may be removed entirely and a mound may be made over the row. In a short time, the leaves will force their way through the mound, and the stalks will be bleached and ready for use. Two or three crops may be gathered from strong roots.

Another way to secure well-bleached chicory will be to remove the roots from the soil during December and place them in a deep box, working some garden soil among them at the same time. Place about eight or ten strong roots to the square foot of box. The box should be about a foot higher than the crown of these plants. Now, by applying a gentle bottom heat, new leaves will be thrown out rapidly, and as soon as these reach a length of eight or ten inches they will be ready for use, provided the box has been covered to keep the light out.

SPINACH.

In the North, this plant is grown largely for greens, but it does not stand shipping to a distant market very well, so it will not come into general favor in the Lower South.

A warm loam should be selected and this fertilized heavily. The plowing need not be deep, and a top dressing of chemical fertilizer after the plants have been started, will be found advantageous.

Make the rows about two feet apart, and drop a seed about every inch; cover with about an inch of soil. Sow in September or October. Thin the plants out to from six to twelve inches in the row according to the variety.

FIG. 7.

Fig. 7 represents a spinach plant ready to be cut for greens. Plants may be used when they are farther advanced than the figure represents.

Cultivate with a wheel-hoe or some other shallow-running cultivator. The main work will be to keep weeds down and the soil moist.

Marketing may be done in the ordinary vegetable crate, but the product must be thoroughly dry before it is packed. Cut the plants so as to leave only about an inch of root; shake the dirt off well, remove all dried or otherwise worthless leaves, and pack in tightly. With our increased facilities for transportation, we may be able to supply many of the Southern markets.

There are not many varieties to choose from; the one known as the Round Leaved is quite common; the Improved Curled American Savoy is also grown extensively. Round Seeded and Prickly Seeded are also sold.

FERTILIZER FORMULA.

Nitrogen .... 3 per cent.
Potash .... 5 per cent.
Available phosphoric acid .... 7 per cent.

Use 800 to 1,200 pounds of the above fertilizer per acre. Apply in the row.

The following table gives the amounts of different fertilizer material necessary to obtain the desired quantity of each element:

Element.	Pounds of different material for one acre.
Nitrogen...............	400 to 600 lbs. cotton-seed meal; or 240 to 360 lbs. dried blood; or 200 to 300 lbs. nitrate of soda; or 150 to 250 lbs. sulphate of ammonia.
Potash...............	320 to 480 lbs. kainit; or 80 to 120 lbs. muriate of potash; or 80 to 120 lbs. sulphate of potash; or 160 to 250 lbs. sulphate of potash and sulphate of magnesia.
Phosphoric acid..	800 to 1,200 lbs. acid phosphate; or 550 to 800 lbs. dissolved bone.

BORICOLE OR KALE.

This vegetable, like several others, has not been grown for the distant market. It is used quite extentensively in New York, Chicago, and several other cities with a large foreign population. It is not probable that we shall ever adapt our taste to liking this vegetable, but it would doubtless pay to raise it in a small way for the palates of those who choose to pay for the trouble. The cities named above would consume hundreds of crates of it at a fair price if offered early enough. It should be brought into these markets during March and April, or even earlier.

Prepare the land as for lettuce and fertilize as for cauliflower.

The seed may be sown in drills during October and November, or it may be sown in cold-frames like cauliflower during November. When the plants have the fourth or fifth leaf, they may be transplanted in the same way as cauliflower.

The large varieties are cut and shipped in barrels; for shipping a long distance or a large amount, crates will be found preferable.

The working of the field is similar to that for the cauliflower; and it should be remembered that the smaller varieties require less space than the larger.

The leading varieties are Siberian and Green Curled. This is only a small part of the varieties grown in Europe. The former variety is also called "Sprouts" in New York market, but this name is also applied to a different vegetable.

CELERY.

There are many reports of success in celery-growing in the South. The profit in this line of vegetable-growing depends largely upon individual tact. In Northern sections, as about Kalamazoo, Mich., and New York, it is raised as a second crop, but we have to raise it as a first crop.

SOIL.

The South has enough excellent celery land to supply the market of the United States. In choosing a plot, two points must be kept in mind. First, the most important, the soil must be rich, not in humus alone, but in *phosphoric acid* and *potash* also; second, the soil must be moist and well drained. Much of our drained muck land has failed to produce celery because it was too dry. Again, some has failed because the essential elements were not well balanced, and hence the soil was not really fertile. Again, some muck land was too new, and caused the crop to "rust" and decay. Celery-raising pays, because it takes more brains to raise it than many other crops do.

PREPARATION OF THE SOIL.

In Northern celery-growing sections, a crop of early vegetables is taken from the land, and then the celery is planted. The land, having received a heavy application of manure before the early vegetables are planted, is not fertilized again unless some thoroughly rotted compost can be obtained. Fresh or undecomposed manure causes a rusting of the vegetable that unfits it for market. The old way of growing celery was to prepare the land well and deeply, and then make trenches six to eight inches deep, and set the plants in these trenches. This method is not followed now by the best celery-growers.

Let us suppose that we have control of a field of drained muck land. The way to proceed will be, first, to make the soil sweet and then plant the crop. Muck land will not be fit to plant the crop on for two or three years after it has been reclaimed. One of the best crops to prepare the land for vegetables is corn; this is quite exhaustive, but the roots penetrate the soil well, and corn is able to stand more sourness than many other crops. Rye and oats prepare the upper stratum well, but their roots do not penetrate the soil so deeply as that of corn. When the soil has become perfectly homogeneous, and the vegetable matter thoroughly incorporated, we may feel quite sure that it is in good condition for celery. It is advisable to test the land by planting out a short row of celery, the year before, on a typical portion; the growth of this will tell for a certainty whether the soil is in good condition. When the soil is in good condition, plow the land deeply, harrow it thoroughly, and remove all rubbish. Before plowing, all corn stalks, large weeds, sticks, and anything else that may interfere with cultivation, should be removed.

If it is a pine woods land that is to be put into condition, the land must be cleared of all woody matter. The rows are then laid off, and a double furrow plowed out deeply; as deep as possible with a two-horse plow. Scatter in this furrow thoroughly decomposed compost of muck and stable manure, at the rate of about a two-horse load to a hundred feet of furrow. Mix the soil and compost thoroughly, gradually filling the furrow in doing so. It is true that celery will grow and produce good looking specimens without any vegetable matter being added, but it is of such quality as would not compete with the Northern-grown article.

SEED-SOWING.

The seed is sown in July or August, preferably in a cold frame or in a plant-bed, where the young plants can be watered easily and protected from the hot sun. If the plant-bed or cold frame has been used before, new fertilizer must be added before the seed is sown. If a new plant-bed has to be made, follow the directions given for the preparation of these on a former page. Put a considerable emphasis on the use of plenty of fertilizer; a pound of the formula given may be used to every six square feet as a fair allowance. Do not put the bed near trees to secure shade from them; they will exhaust the soil before the plants are ready to be transplanted.

When the bed is level and smooth, use a six or eight inch board to mark off the rows. Lay the board down and mark along one side with a dibber, make the drill about half an inch deep and sow the seed in it; turn the board over and make a second drill, and sow this, and so on until the bed is sown. The seed should be scattered thinly, about four to the inch. The plants should be thinned to about an inch apart, when the leaves begin to form. Care should be exercised to keep the weeds out by cultivating and weeding.

A celery bed should be cultivated at least every week, and while the weeds are still in the seed-leaves, they should be weeded out. If the plants tend to become spindly, shear the tops off and the leaves will grow stocky. The leaves that were sheared off would have been lost any way. Crowding the plants in the row makes them send out a strong down-growing root that might be called a tap-root. If the plants are not

CELERY. 75

crowded, the roots spread out upon the surface, and are constantly subject to slight droughts. In the case of a strong central root system, the plant is nourished from the portion of the soil that is constantly moist. Another decided advantage is that the plants may be transplanted with less injury to the root system.

TRANSPLANTING.

Fine plants for transplanting are offered for sale every year at such a low price that it is difficult to see where the profit to the plant-grower comes from. However cheap plants may be in the market, it is preferable to grow your own plants and your own seed. It, however, happens sometimes, through the neglect or carelessness of the employees, that celery plants must be bought or the crop abandoned for that year.

If one has to buy plants from a distance, the land must be entirely ready to receive the plants when they arrive. If it happens to be a dry spell, the plants must be put into a bed where they can be shaded and water in abundance be supplied. A quantity of the plants can then be set out, from time to time, as one is able to take care of them. The setting out must not be delayed, for the plants will soon form roots from the reserve material within themselves; and if this has to be done the second time, it will be a severe draft on the plant. If one has raised his own plants, he may delay transplanting for weeks, awaiting a rain. If the land is in perfect readiness, as soon as the plants are large enough, which will be in October or November, they can be set out at the proper time. A good time to transplant is when the leaf-stalks are three inches long, but fine celery has been raised when they were nearly six inches long.

The distance between the rows is three or four feet,

according to the variety, putting the plants five or six inches apart in the row. Have the soil mellow and deep; stretch a line, and use a dibber for planting. The surface of the land should be even and level. Cut off the tips of the roots; if they are quite long, one-third of them can be cut off to advantage. Cut the leaves back about the same proportion. Place the plant into the hole made by the dibber, and press the ground around it firmly. Mr. T. Greiner says: "If you want to know if your work is done quite right, take a good hold of one of the leaves and pull. If the plant comes out of the ground, it was not firmly set; if the leaf breaks without loosening the plant, all is right." In our sandy loam, we have to be a little more moderate, but the soil must be pressed firmly to the plant. In setting out, put the bud even with the surface of the ground. The work of setting out can be facilitated by cutting the roots and leaves to the proper size before taking to the field. A strong boy may be employed to hand the plants out in good shape to the one doing the setting out.

After setting, the plants must be watered unless the setting out is done immediately after a rain. After watering, as soon as the water has soaked into the ground, rake a thin layer of dry soil over what has been moistened. If it is after a rain, work the ground lightly to give some loose soil on top. These directions, if followed out, will do much to conserve the moisture.

A few days before transplanting, the plants should be hardened off to lessen the shock of transplanting. After having set the plants out, they should be shaded to accustom them to the field gradually. The best device for this is an eight or ten-inch board placed obliquely over the row. The board is secured by stakes, which are driven on the south side of the row, and slanting toward the north; by leaning a board against these, the plants will stand in the shade during the hotter portion of the day, and be exposed to the sun in the evening and morning.

Celery receives the greater portion of its cultivation in the seed-bed. It is cultivated once or twice after setting out, and then the earth is gradually drawn up to the row, keeping the foliage on top of an A-shaped ridge. In the family garden, this is made with a common hoe, but on celery farms special plows are used for this purpose; these are drawn by a team, and hill both sides at once. This banking is for the purpose of blanching. This is simply to keep chlorophyll from forming in the stems, and to remove what has already formed.

Shutting out the light in many other ways is just as good as banking or hilling, if it keeps the light out as thoroughly. Another way of bleaching (or blanching) that is employed extensively is to use boards in the place of earth. Eight to twelve-inch boards are taken, according to the variety of celery to be bleached, and laid flat alongside of the row with one edge next to the plants, raise the outer edge of the boards up against the plants; now move the lower edge out a few inches, this will let the board stand against the row of celery; press the board down to shut out all light from the bottom, and the whole work of banking is done. In two or three weeks the celery will be bleached sufficiently for use. If there is danger of the boards falling, they may be fastened by nailing a light strip from one to the other. The upper edge of the board should be pressed together firmly, but not hard enough to bruise the leaves. This method is good for family use, but when celery is grown on a large scale, it takes too much lumber and too much work.

Among other methods of bleaching are those of putting tile around the plant, and of wrapping with thick paper or covering with a paper tube, but all of these have failed to meet the wants of celery growers.

There are, then, two ways of bleaching celery: First, by banking it with earth; Second, by banking it with boards. The former is preferable when celery is grown on a large scale, and may be accomplished by hand, by a one horse plow, or by a two horse plow. The second method is preferable when celery is grown for family use, when refuse boards can be used, and only a small portion of the crop is wanted from time to time. Later in the season, or when celery has attained its full growth, it takes nearly twice as long to bleach it. This should be borne in mind when it is prepared to meet the wants of a certain time.

THE NEW CELERY CULTURE.

The process is not quite true to name. It could be applied as well to the method of cultivating without using trenches. In short, the new celery culture is simply to cultivate celery with profit when the rows are planted about six inches apart and the plants six inches in the row. The main point in mind when this system was suggested was to do away with the expense of bleaching. Three points must be kept in mind to succeed with this method: First, we must have a variety that is self-bleaching; that is, we must have a variety that makes enough shade to keep the stalks bleached from the time that it is large enough for the market; Second, the soil must be rich enough to support and mature six or eight times the usual crop; Third, there must be moisture enough present to fulfil the same conditions.

In preparing for this method, we should remember how much fertilizer there was used on six or eight acres, and then put a like amount on one acre, and it will be necessary to have some way of supplying moisture. Some system of irrigation is usually necessary.

This method, although it has many warm advocates, has not been tested sufficiently to be recommended without reservation. It has met with sufficient success to warrant thorough trials. The work up to the time of setting out is the same as for the old method, except in regard to the fertilizer. In marking out the land, make checks from 7x7 to 10x10 inches, according to the size of the variety. It must be borne in mind that the foliage must be dense enough to shut out the light as early as the stalks are large enough to market. As soon as the plants shade the ground completely, the work is done; there is no hilling up except around the outside row.

By planting successively from the earliest to the latest varieties, we can have the crop come in during the entire market time, and bank only the outside row of the entire field.

The ordinary method furnishes about 20,000 plants to the acre; this new method, nearly or quite 150,000. Mr. T. Greiner, quoted above, in his "Celery for Profit," makes a comparison of the two methods. He finds the expenses for raising and marketing one acre by the old method, is $260; that of the new process, $920. These figures are about as low as they can be put; for the South, we must add something for additional cost of fertilizer and for transportation; but on the other hand, our land is cheaper, and possibly the labor and plants are cheaper. Now for the profits: On the acre under the ordinary cultivation, it was $190; on the acre by the new culture, it was $1,180. The estimate seems entirely fair; the celery is estimated at 30 cents a dozen bunches, and allows for a loss of about 25 per cent. of the plants set out.

Celery sheds have not been tested sufficiently to be recommended; but where this vegetable is raised on the new plan, it will probably pay. They are constructed like a pineapple shed; posts are set 10 x 10 feet, and stand nine feet above the ground. The tops of the posts are connected by stringers running east and west. On these stringers are placed four-inch battens about four inches apart. This shed cuts off one-half of the sun's rays, and diffuses the remainder so they will not fall heavily on any one place. The battens running north and south distribute the sunlight more evenly than when they run the other way.

IRRIGATION.

In following the new celery culture, it is necessary to resort to irrigation for the water supply. This supply may be distributed in one of two ways—either by open ditches at short intervals, or by running tile near the surface.

When the water is distributed by open ditches, the ditches are cut three to four feet apart. In watering, these are allowed to flow full until the earth is thoroughly soaked, then it is turned into another set, and thus continued until the whole area has been treated. These ditches are shallow, only a few inches deep. On a clayey soil, they are run nearly on the level, but on sandy loam. there must be a considerable decline to have the water reach the further end.

Irrigating by the use of tile, or other more or less solid pipe laid into the soil, is the better plan. This is especially advisable when the water supply is limited, as less is lost by soaking away and from evaporating. In this, as in the open ditches, we have a main supply, and running from this, are the arms that do the feeding or furnishing to the crop.

MARKETING.

There is a rapidly-growing demand for celery in our home market, and judging from the price that it brings to the retail dealers in our State, there must be a large profit to some one, or somewhere a large waste. The many rich people who visit the South during the win-

FIG. 8.

Figure 8 represents a celery plant trimmed and washed, ready to be packed for market.

ter, consume large quantities. These people want the very finest, and are willing to pay a good price for it, while an inferior article will remain on the market, and had usually better be left in the field.

With the increased facilities for transportation, we can put our article in the hands of home consumers in two or three days less time than the New York or Kalamazoo growers can, and this means a preference, even at an advanced price. Consumers want this vegetable crisp, fresh, and free from "strings."

PREPARING FOR MARKET.

Celery is not grown so generally in the South that the local markets are supplied. There are only a few places that produce it at all, and these do so in quantity. It may seem like a small and slow business to train people up to like any vegetable, but a taste for this is easily cultivated. It has been only a few years since gardening for local sales has been profitable in many sections of the South, and in some it is not meeting with success even now. The fault is as much that of the producer as of the buyers. There are a great many reasons why home markets should be cultivated rather than look to New York or other Northern markets, where our celery has to compete with the product from fertile land and cheap fertilizer. The seaboard cities are not good markets for us, as we have to compete with the cheap ocean transportation. We should rather look to some of our inland cities and towns. It is not uncommon to see an inferior grade of celery selling for 10 and 15 cents a bunch at the local markets, and on inquiring, it has been found that this has been shipped from a distance.

In the matter of preparation for market, there seems to be very little choice. The main point is to get it on sale in a crisp form, and to have it sightly; both points are often overlooked, however. In the Northern markets, there are two distinct ways of preparing this vegetable for market. The Kalamazoo shippers make a large bunch of twelve plants; the outer leaves are s'ripped off nicely, and the roots cut very short and square across. These dozen plants are trimmed off nicely and put in a frame and tied, and are then packed in flat crates or boxes and sent to market, either to the Western or Middle States. The Eastern or New England market calls for a little different kind of bunches. For these, the plant must be trimmed to expose the heart to view. From three to five of such plants are then fastened together by driving a nail through the roots, or they may be tied together. Most of the root is left on the plants, making the nailing possible. The size of the plants governs the number to be used in making a bunch. The bunches are then packed in long, narrow crates, so the whole can be inspected from the outside. The New Jersey, Maryland, and Virginia markets usually accept celery packed tightly in boxes or barrels. For the local markets, it is not necessary to use any particular form of package, yet, where one intends to establish a business, some regular form of package or crate should be adopted, as that makes a trade-mark; the crate should be light and tasty. For long distance shipping, a good crate can be made by making a solid bottom of a half or three-fourths inch stuff; a rim around this about four inches high—this portion of the crate should be water-tight; put a one-inch square post in each corner, twelve inches high; nail a strip across each end, and several strips nailed to hold the plants from being removed. Crates of this kind, about two feet square, have been used, but the size may be varied to suit the occasion. Before shipping, moisten the plants well, and do not trim the roots.

To prepare celery for market, two tubs of water are

taken to the field, and as soon as the plants are dug they are plunged into one tub, washed off well, and then into the second to rinse. All the green and partially dried leaves are picked off. If the product is intended for a near market, the roots are cut to suit the trade. For long distance shipping, the roots are left on and moistened after packing.

VARIETIES.

Giant Pascal is said to be the best for the South. Several other varieties have been grown successfully. One will find that most of the good varieties for other sections will do well here. For "new celery culture," use self-bleaching varieties, except White Plume, which cannot be recommended.

FERTILIZER FORMULA.

Available phosphoric acid .... 6 per cent.
Potash .... 8 per cent.
Nitrogen .... 5 per cent.

Use 1,000 to 2,000 pounds of the above fertilizer to the acre. If the celery is planted on muck land, reduce the amount of nitrogen.

The following fertilizer ingredients will give the amount of fertilizer elements designated in the above formula:

Element.	Pounds of different material for one acre.
Nitrogen..	850 to 1,700 lbs. cotton-seed meal; or 500 to 1,000 lbs. dried blood; or 350 to 700 lbs. nitrate of soda; or 250 to 500 lbs. sulphate ammonia.
Potash.........	1,000 to 2,000 lbs. kainit; or 160 to 320 lbs. muriate of potash; or 175 to 350 lbs. sulphate of potash; or 350 to 700 lbs. sulphate of potash and sulphate of magnesia.
Phosphoric acid..	600 to 1,200 lbs. acid phosphate; or 500 to 1,000 lbs. dissolved bone.

CELERIAC.

This vegetable is not grown extensively in America. It has been introduced by some of our population who acquired a taste for it in Europe. It is a near relative of celery, as the first portion of the name indicates.

The seed may be procured from most of our seedsmen at about the same rate that is paid for celery seed. Prepare the seed-bed in the same way as for celery, giving same attention to watering and transplanting. Prepare the field as you would for parsnips or for celery culture after the old method. The plants should be set out when they reach the size of about three inches. If this vegetable is sown during a moist year, it will not be necessary to transplant, and may be sown in the field at once prepared in the same way as for transplanting. The cultivation should be shallow, and at the same time thorough. It is not necessary to hill this vegetable up as in the case of celery, as the roots are used and require no bleaching. In the kitchen, it is prepared much the same as parsnips and turnips.

While this vegetable has no commercial standing, it is easily grown and of such delightful flavor to those who like celery, that it will always be found desirable in the home garden.

CABBAGE.

The season for marketing cabbage is not long, because the Maine and Nova Scotia cabbage will keep until March or April, while the spring crop of North Georgia and South Carolina begins to reach market in June. Some years the Northern crop is small; in such cases, late winter cabbage commands a high price. If at the same time the potato crop is light, there will be a demand for Southern cabbage. Often, the vegetable-growers can anticipate such conditions, and put in a large crop of cabbage. There is a large Southern market that would depend on our cabbage if the supply were constant.

Cabbage is an excellent crop to feed cattle. In some of the dairying districts, it is raised as a second crop with a view of feeding to milch cows.

PLANT-BED.

This is probably the easiest vegetable to grow from seed that we have in market. It is not necessary to have a cold-frame to start the seedlings, but success is more certain by using it. The bed used to raise the seedlings need not have bottom heat, and need not be as fertile as for most other seedlings. To produce stocky plants, it is better to have the bed rather cool. If one discovers that the plants are not progressing rapidly enough to bring them to the size desired by transplanting time, they can be stimulated to rapid growth by the use of some liquid manure, or cotton-seed meal. The latter must not come in contact with the plants, as it is liable to cause a "damping off" in the seed-bed when it begins to decay. One-half to an ounce of seed should give plants enough for an acre.

VARIETIES.

There is practically no killing frost for this vegetable in the Lower South; consequently, it is found more profitable to raise the larger kinds. Charleston Wakefield (see Figure 9), Premium Flat Dutch, and Louisville Drumhead are favorites in various portions, but

FIG. 9.

Figure 9 represents a Charleston Wakefield cabbage ready to cut for distant market. One or two more circles of leaves may be removed without disadvantage. When cabbage is high priced, this has been trimmed sufficiently.

FIG. 10.

these varieties should be grown only to medium size. For family use, when cabbage is wanted in as short time as possible, Jersey Wakefield (see Figure 10) or Early Winningstadt are desirable varieties.

SOWING THE SEED.

It is preferable to sow the seed in drills, far enough apart to permit them to be worked either by hoe or hand-plow. In our, latitude, September or October, depending upon the variety, is the right time to sow for February, March and April markets of the North. This will bring the crop into market after the Northern stored crop has been consumed, and before the early spring crop has matured. The drills are made about three-fourths of an inch deep. As soon as the seedlings begin to break through the ground, make a liberal application of tobacco dust; repeat the dusting every three or four days. This will kill or drive away some insects that are quite numerous at this time of the year.

If the seeds grow well, the plants will become crowded in the drills before they attain their third leaf. Cabbage seedlings may be transplanted at any time in their growth, without loosing any plants, hence, we should transplant them to a new bed as soon as they show signs of crowding. They should be transplanted to the field before the height of six inches is reached. If the plants grow too rapidly, they may be checked by withholding the water or by shifting them to a new bed.

SOIL.

Cabbage is a gross feeder, and will succeed on soil where many other crops fail. The soil for ordinary gardening is considered excellent for this vegetable. If the land is not level, a northern slope is preferred, as that is cooler and keeps a more nearly constant temperature, but the northern districts need a southern slope. Large cabbage will stand 15° F. without being killed, but that which is recently set out, needs some light protection. Seedlings or plants in the seed-bed can stand about 20° F., but if they are in rapid growth, this temperature makes their leaves look as if they had been scalded,

CABBAGE.

FERTILIZER FORMULA.

Available phosphoric acid .....7 per cent.
Potash ....8 per cent.
Nitrogen ....5 per cent.

Use 1,500 to 2,500 pounds of the above formula to the acre.

The following table will give the amounts of different substances it will require to make the amounts of the fertilizer elements called for in the foregoing table.

Element.	Pounds of different material for one acre.
Nitrogen	1,200 to 2,000 lbs. cotton-seed meal; or 750 to 1,200 lbs. dried blood; or 500 to 800 lbs. nitrate of soda; or 400 to 650 lbs. sulphate of ammonia.
Potash	1,200 to 1,600 lbs. kainit; or 300 to 400 lbs. muriate potash; or 300 to 400 lbs. sulphate potash; or 550 to 750 lbs. sulphate of potash and sulphate of magnesia.
Phosphoric acid	1,000 to 1,750 lbs. acid phosphate; or 800 to 1,500 lbs. dissolved bone.

PLANTING AND CULTIVATING.

Before transplanting, it is well to harden the plants off, and, when ready to remove them, soak the ground thoroughly; this will cause more soil to adhere to the roots. A rainy time is preferable for planting out, and this can usually be waited for, though it is really not necessary, as the plants grow very readily. For medium to large varieties, make the rows three feet apart, and put the plants two to three feet apart in the row. They should be planted with a view of doing all the cultivating by horse power. If the season happens to be dry, be sure to give frequent and thorough cultivation, to conserve the moisture of the soil.

PREPARING FOR MARKET.

It often happens that much rain falls when the heads have become solid, causing them to burst. This may be prevented by running a plow with a long sweep on one side of the row to cut off most of the roots. The bursting is caused by an assimilation of too much moisture, and a consequent expansion of the heart while the outer leaves cannot stretch sufficiently.

For shipping, nearly all the outer leaves are stripped off, leaving just enough to protect the head; the stalk is then cut off about even. The heads should be gathered dry, and kept so until they reach their destination. If somewhat wilted when received by the retail dealer, they may be placed in a cellar, or other moist place, when they will become crisp and fresh again.

Cabbage may be classed among the staple products, so people are not very notional about how it appears on the market. While it is an easy crop to grow, there are, on the other hand, a great many failures.

MARKETING.

There is no settled form of package for cabbage. The smaller early cabbage is usually crated or barreled; the fall cabbage is sometimes shipped in bulk, especially when sold by the car-load. Barrels are frequently used, when only a few are to be shipped to one address. Crates are often seen on the markets of large cities; they are about 2x4 by 4 or 5. In Florida, cabbage crates are made to hold a hundred pounds—smaller than the dimensions given above.

SPROUTS.

This vegetable is like cabbage in many respects, but in place of growing one large head, it produces many small ones on the side of a stalk. While the English prize it highly, most Americans have never eaten it. There is no extensive market for it. The tuft of leaves growing terminally may be eaten, but the small heads at the side of the stalk produce the delicious portions. These heads are prepared much as cabbage or cauliflower, but will be found to have a different flavor from either.

Prepare the land just as for cabbage, but sow the seed in the field where the crop is to grow. The seed must be sown thick enough to feed all insects on that and the adjoining plots, as they usually appear to be extra severe on crops that one does not wish to transplant. When the plants are about six inches high, they may be thinned out to eighteen inches in the row.

In the matter of fertilizing, cultivation and time of sowing, follow that given for cabbage.

FIG. 11.

Figure 11 represents a "Sprouts plant" trimmed to show the "sprouts." The leaves may be used as a substitute for collards, and the sprouts used as cabbage or cauliflower.

CAULIFLOWER.

This vegetable is much more delicate than cabbage, though it partakes largely of its nature. It tastes somewhat like cabbage, but has a flavor of its own that is most highly and delightfully developed in the most perfect specimens.

As a money crop for the South, it can be recommended to all sections. It is much more difficult to raise than cabbage, and consequently brings a larger profit to those who are able to grow it successfully It has been grown successfully in all sections of the Lower South, so we need not hesitate on that line, and as thousands of acres are raised annually on Long Island, we see that difficulties connected with raising it is not an obstacle to the average gardeners. Cauliflower is imported from France, and sold at a high figure during late winter and early spring.

SEED SOWING.

In sections where the temperature does not go below 18°F., this crop can be relied upon for February and March delivery. If the crop is wanted for these months, the seed should be sown in a cold frame during September and October.

Rake the cold frame off smoothly and if it is not already fertile, it should receive a liberal application of commercial fertilizer. This should be worked in thoroughly and allowed to stand a week or ten days before the seed is sown. Cotton-seed meal or other vegetable matter should not be used at this time of year, as it propagates diseases which destroy seedling cauliflower. During winter this form of fertilizer can be used in the cold frames with safety. Cotton-seed meal and other vegetable matter should be composted and thoroughly rotted before using it in cold frames. Make drills three or four inches apart and three-quarters of an inch deep. Sow the seed in by hand. A convenient aid may be made by punching a nail-hole in the bottom of an old fruit-can. The size of the hole should be tested by sowing on some canvas or plant-cloth. A seeder may be used with profit if one has much seed to sow. The seed when sown should be covered with about three quarters of an inch of soil.

The soil should be kept moist by frequent applications of water—never use enough to soak the bed, and on the other hand, do not allow the soil to become dry. As soon as the seedlings appear, watering may be less frequent and heavier. The surface of the cold frame should become dry so as to prevent damping off. If, at any time, it is noticed that some plants are falling over, as if cut off, and yet are not cut off, it is very suspicious. An application of dust or dry sand will often be found of advantage.

As soon as the seedlings are an inch or an inch and a half high, they should be transplanted to rows four inches apart and about an inch in the row. Use only the finest seedlings and destroy the poorer ones. This transplanting discards the poorer seedlings, and gives the stronger ones greater advantage, and at the same time it reduces the danger from damping off. From the time that the seedlings begin to appear, dust the surface of the bed with tobacco dust. The dusting should be most liberal along the drill, and should be done an hour or two after watering; repeat it every three or four days.

As soon as the plants begin to crowd in the rows, they should be transplanted again. This time set the plants four by four inches. In six or eight weeks, the plants are ready to go to the field. Care must be exercised that the plants do not remain in the cold frame too long, as leggy plants are liable to "shoot up" to seed without making fine heads.

SOIL.

A rather heavy, sandy soil, in a warm location, is preferable for winter marketing, but for late spring market a heavier and cooler soil will give a larger yield.

Prepare the land deeply and thoroughly. If some crop has been used for soiling, the material should be plowed in early enough to incorporate it well with the soil before planting time.

The fertilizer should be applied along the row, and worked in thoroughly. From several days to two weeks should be allowed to pass before

SETTING OUT.

Make the rows two and a half to three feet apart, and set the plants eighteen inches or two feet apart in the row.

If a rain does not occur at the time, it will be necessary to water, as we cannot wait for a rain, as in the cabbage, but the plants must go out, as they are liable to be too large and a portion of the crop be worthless.

CULTIVATION.

The general care and cultivation is like that for early cabbage. When the heads reach the size of a tea cup, the leaves may be tied over them to keep from becoming green. This is not always necessary, nor is it always followed.

CUTTING.

After this vegetable has begun to head, it requires a good deal of judgment to put it into the market properly. The field must be picked over repeatedly, and the matured heads removed, or they will spoil.

CAULIFLOWER.

If the weather is warm, they are liable to spot, and this makes them unfit for market. To examine a head, part the leaves and see if it is beginning to crack; if so, remove it. In case the leaves have been tied over the head to bleach it, the leaves must be parted on the side to keep the sun from getting in. In cutting, a good strong knife with a blade about eight inches long is needed. Cut the stalk so as to leave about two circles of leaves. (See Fig. 12.) If the product is first class, it will pay to cut the stalk below the leaves and cart the crop to the packing-house.

CRATING.

Trim off all but the inner circle of leaves, cut the stalks off near the leaves and wrap in a thin pa-

FIG. 12.

Figure 12 represents a head of cauliflower with the last circle of leaves remaining. For ordinary markets these are pressed over its head and packed. For fancy market these are cut off and head wrapped in tissue paper.

per. In the fancy markets, nearly as much pains is taken with this vegetable as with fancy fruits, and the growing of this class of cauliflower pays best. Before wrapping, each head should be allowed to dry thoroughly. In the matter of package, the customers are not so particular because the product is usually removed from it before it is sold to the retail dealers. The barrel or box should not contain more than two and one-half bushels, to avoid bruising the lower heads by the weight of the upper ones. For a distant market, it is better to use a crate that will hold about as much as a tomato-crate.

The seed is imported from Europe; only a small quantity being grown in this country. It is quite difficult to grow the seed in the gardening districts of the United States, as the heads have to be kept over-winter and the seed grown the next summer. Fine heads cannot be kept from rotting, so half matured specimens have to be chosen. This degenerates the kind in a few generations.

Is not here a profitable employment for a small capital? Our crop can be matured so the seed can grow the same season. If a crop happened to be somewhat late, it might be allowed to go to seed. With a decrease in the price of seed, there would be an increase in consumption. As it is one of the most delicious vegetables, there need be no fear of over production.

VARIETIES.

Early Erfurt, Snowball, and Extra Early Paris (see Fig. 12), are good, and can be depended upon for a crop. There are other varieties coming into common use, but these three have the lead.

The price of the seed is one great drawback on cauliflower raising.

FERTILIZER FORMULA.

Available phosphoric acid......7 per cent.
Potash ....8 per cent.
Nitrogen ....5 per cent.

Use about 1,500 pounds of the above formula. For table of ingredients to use per acre, refer to that topic under cabbage.

BROCOLI.

Nicholson, in the *Dictionary of Gardening*, considers this as "A cultivated variety of cabbage, having the young infloresence changed into a fleshy, edible head." It is hardier than cauliflower and keeps well, but is not so choice a vegetable, so does not sell as well. Some of the varieties are often confused with cauliflower in new markets.

Sow the seed in a cold frame during September, or in Southern Georgia in December or January. As soon as the seedlings are an inch high, prick them out and transfer. Make the rows four inches apart and set the seedlings an inch in the row. Press the soil about their roots lightly and water thoroughly. A speedy way of setting them out is to make a drill about half inch deep and place the seedlings in this in an upright position, then press the soil to them from both sides. After a portion of a cold frame has been set out apply an abundance of water with a very fine spray. By separating the plants this way, damping off, that often creates sad havoc among plants belonging to the cabbage tribe, is largely checked. As soon as the plants begin to crowd again, reset them so as to give more room; this time set the plants four inches in the row, leaving the rows the same distance apart as before. When the plants are four or five inches high they should be set in the field.

In the districts where the orange grows, the seeding should be repeated every three weeks until the first of January or February; north of that district sow every three weeks until the first of February.

The soil should be rich sandy loam. Prepare it deeply and fertilize heavily. Lay the rows off three feet apart and plant eighteen inches apart in the row.

As soon as the first seeding of plants are ready to set out they should be hardened off for a day or two only and planted in the field. If a cold snap is just at hand the plants may be kept in the frame for a week or two longer. A fresh supply of plants should always be kept under special protection, to be used in case of a hard freeze that may kill the plants in the field.

Cultivate frequently, but only to a medium depth. When the heads are maturing a light band of bast or other cheap material may be used to tie the leaves over them for the purpose of bleaching.

FIG. 13.

When mature, cut the heads, leaving only a few leaves on to protect (see Fig. 13), and pack tightly in a vegetable crate.

The leading varieties are Veitch's Self-protecting, Purple Cape and White Cape.

Fertilizer formula and fertilizer should be the same as for Cauliflower.

COLLARDS.

This is decidedly an American vegetable, grown almost exclusively for Southern markets by people of the South. As a money crop it is nothing grand, yet it may be marketed when vegetables are usually scarce. Those who have cultitvated a taste for it will refuse cabbage and cauliflower at the same price. Why should we not have a special liking for some vegetable which others regard as strong and otherwise unfit to eat. Many other great countries have their favorite dish that we don't crave; the Welshman prefers flag; the French, artichoke (Loan); the Spaniard, garlic; and so on, not even to mention countries that pay a handsome price for bird's-nests. We make no apology whatever for preferring collards.

Select a rich loam, fertilize heavily, and prepare deeply. Follow the dirctions given for the preparation of land for cabbage.

Sow the seed in a cold frame or in open bed during February and March in the orange belt, and as late as August in Virginia. As soon as the plants begin to crowd one another, shift to a new place in the cold frame. When the plants are from four to six inches high, plant in the field. Lay the rows off four feet apart and put the plants three feet in the row.

The crop may be marketed any time after the first of October. This may be done in crates, in barrels or in bulk.

FERTILIZER FORMULA.

Nitrogen... ...4 per cent.
Available phosphoric acid .....7 per cent.
Potash... ......9 per cent.

VEGETABLE GROWING.

FERTILIZER.

Element.	Pounds per acre.	Pounds of different material for one acre.
Nitrogen...	40 to 80	2000 to 4000 lbs. of muck; or 500 to 1000 lbs. of cotton-seed meal; or 250 to 500 lbs. of nitrate of soda; or 400 to 800 lbs. of dried blood; or 200 to 400 lbs. of sulphate ammonia.
Phos. acid.	70 to 140	500 to 1000 lbs. of dissolved bone; or 700 to 1400 lbs. of bone meal; or 600 to 1200 lbs. of acid phosphate.
Potash......	90 to 180	180 to 360 lbs. of muriate; or 180 to 360 lbs. of sulphate; or 700 to 1400 lbs. of kainit.

KOHL-RABI.

Plants belonging to the mustard family have gone through many queer contortions to supply the people of Europe with vegetables. Cabbage stores the nourishment in abundant leaves; turnips store the food material in the roots; kohl-rabi splits the difference and stores the nourishment in the stem, at the base of the leaves and above the root. In the matter of taste, there is displayed the same adaptation, for, while it partakes of the flavor of cabbage and of turnips, it is distinct from both (see Fig. 14). It is prepared for eating in the same way as turnips.

Sow the seed in a cold frame in September and repeat the sowing every four weeks until the first of February. As soon as the seedlings are an inch high, and before the leaves begin to appear, prick them out, and plant in rows four inches apart; set the plants an inch in the row. As soon as they begin to crowd in the row, transfer again; when the plants are four or five inches high, plant out in the field. The soil should be a rich loam prepared deeply. Make the rows two feet apart and set the plants a foot in the row. Cultivate often to a medium depth. As soon as they have attained a diameter of two inches they may be used. Some varieties are grown to feed to stock; these will be found to be coarse for table use when full grown, but are good when half grown.

FIG. 14.

This vegetable has not been shipped and will probably not be of value for this purpose.

ONION.

Of all the crops that we grow there is none that requires more attention in the manipulation of the land previous to planting than this one does. A strong reason why this vegetable is not more largely raised in the South for market is, that so many people do not go into vegetable growing with the view of sticking to it. In the onion-growing districts, land is said to improve with each crop that is removed from it. Land that has been cropped for twenty years is raising better crops now than the neighboring land that is just being cleared for that purpose.

SOIL.

A sandy loam, with a clay subsoil, will give excellent returns, provided there is an abundance of humus or other nitrogenous matter present. Most of our land is subject to too great a variation in the moisture it contains. The roots of the onions do not enter the soil deeply, so they are easily affected by changes in the upper stratum.

PREPARING THE LAND.

In selecting a plot of land, be sure to take one that does not become soggy in wet weather nor dry during a drought. If the right kind of land is not at hand, some should be bought that is all right—not rented, unless one can have the option of buying it at a fair price. One should not go into onion-raising as a temporary employment, unless he be an onion grower from some other section—and these need no advice. Where it is possible to have an artesian well or other constant supply of water, it will be found profitable to irrigate. The land should be well drained. Put the underdrains close together, so as to remove the surplus water quickly.

The land should be shallow but thoroughly plowed, leaving no particle unturned. Remove all roots or sticks, or other debris, before plowing and again after plowing, then harrow thoroughly, removing every particle in the form of sticks or straw; even the roots of last year's grass should be removed. After the land has been thus thoroughly prepared, it should be allowed to remain two weeks or so before fertilizing, when it should be stirred again.

SEED.

The Bermuda is recommended as being the best variety for a crop in the South. There seems to be a good deal of difficulty in obtaining genuine seed. This is a very important point in the success of onion-growing. There is probably no other crop where so much depends on obtaining a good strain of seed. It is not profitable to use old seed when new can be obtained.

SEED-BED.

The seed should be sown in seed beds, or cold frames, prepared with special care. These may be prepared a month or so before hand, and should be worked over frequently to have the fertilizer incorporated into the soil. These seed-beds must be constructed so the moisture in them can be controlled.

If the seed-bed is free from weed-seed, as it should be, the rows may be made about three inches apart, and the seed sown thick enough to raise about three thousand plants to one linear foot (six square feet) of standard cold frame. This will give 500 to 750 plants to a row six feet long. There is considerable variation in the number of plants that can be produced from an ounce of seed; good gardeners are able to produce

5,000. There are so many elements that enter into the question that the number cannot be exact. When the seed is cared for properly, it will give plants in six weeks that are large enough to be set out. They should be set out before they are as large as a thin lead pencil.

TIME TO SOW.

As in the case of potatoes, one should watch the Northern markets and crops. If onions are selling for a very small price in the fall, it is clearly not wise to plant a large crop for early spring, but seeding time should be delayed a month or two. A good crop never fails to bring a fair return; it is quite unusual to sell any portion of the crop in the South for less than a dollar a bushel.

The seed may be sown any time from the first of September to first of January. The last date brings it into competition with the crops raised in the section just north of us, but the price is not low enough usually to make the crop cease to be profitable. October is a favorite date, and one that brings the crop into market after the stored crop has been consumed. Immediately after the seed has been sown in the cold frame the preparation of the field should be commenced.

FERTILIZING.

Good compost or well-rotted barn-yard manure will be found excellent, and guano still better. Whatever kind be used, be sure that it contains no weed seed. If both home-made and commercial fertilizer are to be used, plow the former in, and after the land has been well worked down, use the latter broadcast, and mix it with the soil by using a cut-away harrow. In the matter of using fertilizer, Mr. Gaitskill's advice to the Florida State Horticultural Society should be followed.

ONION. 105

When discussing the amount of fertilizer to use on vegetables, he said; "Put on all you think the land can stand, then put on as much more, and you will have about half enough."

FERTILIZER FORMULA.

Phosphoric acid, available..... 6 per cent.
Potash. .... 9 per cent.
Nitrogen .. .. 5 per cent.

Use a ton of this on land that is considered fertile enough for an ordinary crop; two tons may be applied on land that has been cropped several years.

AMOUNTS OF FERTILIZERS.

Element.	Pounds. per acre.	Pounds of different material for one acre.
Nitrogen...	100-200	1600 to 3000 lbs. cotton-seed meal; or 700 to 1400 lbs. nitrate of soda; or 1000 to 2000 lbs. dried blood; or 1400 to 2800 lbs. guano;* or 500 to 1000 lbs. sulphate of ammonia.
Potash......	180-330	2200 to 4400 lbs. kainit; or 360 to 720 lbs. muriate of potash; or 350 to 700 lbs. sulphate of potash; or 700 to 1400 lbs. sulphate of potash and sulphate of magnesia.
Phos. acid.	120-240	1200 to 2400 lbs. acid phosphate; or 1000 to 2000 lbs. dissolved bone.

SETTING OUT.

The most expensive operation in the growing of onions in this way is the setting out. This will be found to cost about $40 an acre. Boys and girls will set out 2,000 to 3,000 a day; a good man can set 4,000 to 5,000, and as it takes about 160,000 plants to an acre, it will be seen that it is no small job. It is claimed by persons who have set out several acres

---

*When guano is used as a source of nitrogen only two-thirds the quantities given as a source of potash will be required, and only half the quantities of phosphoric acid. This is due to the fact that guano contains a large amount of potash and phosphoric acid.

that they can do so at the cost of $20 per acre. Persons who are not familiar with onion growing will consider this an almost insurmountable obstacle, but when we remember that it does away with the early weeding and hoeing, the expense will not be so heavy as it is first supposed. Twenty dollars is not sufficient to bring an acre of onions to four weeks old by the old method, and have the field free from weeds.

After the seedlings have grown large enough to be handled easily, they should be transplanted. Mark the rows off about twelve inches apart, if they are to be worked by hand; if by horse-power, the rows must be from tewnty to twenty-four inches apart. A simple rake-like contrivance that has teeth at proper intervals will serve the purpose of a marker. If the marker is wide enough to mark out six or eight rows at once, it will be found steadier than a small one. All that is necessary is to make a mark for a guide; the lines or marks need not be deep or broad. A revolving marker may be made by fastening a thin rope around a wooden roller and inserting pegs at proper intervals on the circumference; it will lay off distances and be a good guide in planting. If the pegs have been put so they will make a dot every twelve inches in the row, all that is necessary is to set a plant in each dot, and then put three between. These dots are especially desirable if one has boys and girls at work.

For setting the plants a small, flat dibber is used; a home-made one will serve the purpose as well as any. A piece of seasoned hard wood, one inch square and six long, should be shaved down to a flat point, and a handle fixed across the top. Such a tool can be made easily and quickly, or one may have a steel one made by a blacksmith; these will be found better, but where a good many hands are being worked, the item of expense will be well worth considering.

To set the plant, insert the dibber on the line and press it from you; set the plant with the other hand; remove the dibber, and set it in the ground beyond, and press the soil firmly to the plant. This operation ensures that the soil will be pressed firmly about the roots of the plants. The plants must be set perpendicularly, or an ill-shaped onion will result. When one has many hands at work, they should be divided into squads, and each placed under a careful foreman, who should see that the work is done properly and keep the planters supplied with sets.

The seedlings may be removed from the bed by passing a trowel under the row and lifting a lot of them at once; then separate from the soil, and trim off the long roots and leaves. The leaves are in the way of later cultivation and the roots bother in planting.

If the roots do not start off readily, and the conditions of temperature and moisture are all right, a light dressing of nitrate of soda will be found valuable. Mr. T. Greiner advises the use of seventy-five pounds of nitrate of soda to the acre. Make one application as soon as the field has been set out; and a repetition of this about every ten days, until five applications have been given. If this is done when the plants are free from dew and rain, there will be no difficulty from scalding the foliage. It should not be carried on too long, as it will keep the onions growing after they should have ripened; this same difficulty will be experienced if one uses a fertilizer containing an unusual amount of nitrogen, or if one uses a complete fertilizer on muck land.

CULTIVATION.

"Tillage is manure," is an old and true saying, but in cultivating onions we must be careful that it is done properly. There are just two points to be kept in mind: the first is to keep the weeds down, and the second is to conserve the moisture in the soil. The former of these is well understood by all gardeners, and needs but to be mentioned; the second, however, is usually overlooked; many people recognize the value of working land during dry times, but do not know why it has the desired effect on the crop. At least an inch of loose soil should be kept on the ground as a mulch during dry times.

For hand cultivation, the double wheel-hoe is undoubtedly the best machine now on the market. Whatever tool is used, it should not penetrate the ground more than an inch, and in no case touch the bulbs of the plants.

If the field is to be cultivated by horse-power, it will require a plow made especially for that purpose; there is no difficulty in training a horse or mule to do the work well, and a great deal of hard work can be avoided by using one. In the onion growing sections, the land is too costly to permit the use of a horse, so the wheel-hoes are used exclusively.

The workers in the field carry a bag with them to receive any purslane or other plant that may have been missed or allowed to grow to flowering size. All large weeds are carried to the edge of the field and thrown in heaps to rot. There are a very few fields that are free enough of weed seed to grow a crop without some hand weeding; this should be done with a knife —*i. e.*, large weeds should not be pulled when growing in the row. For this purpose there are knives made, which may be obtained from most supply stores, but an old case-knife may be bent into good shape without costing as much. The point is turned up to lessen the danger of hacking into the plant as it is being used.

The ordinary garden-hoes do not work well in the onion fields; a wornout one that has been cut down to one half its width, so as to leave the corners acute, will work pretty well. All tools should be kept as sharp as the steel will permit; a dull hoe will soon use up more time than would pay for a new one.

THE OLD PLAN.

The primitive method of raising onions is to grow the seed in the field where the crop is to grow. This method is still followed in many onion-growing sections. Prepare the land in the same way as you would for setting out. Sowing is best done by a seed-drill. Set the drill so it will sow from twelve to thirty-six seed to the linear foot, according to the variety and the germinating quality of the seed. Make the rows from fifteen to twenty inches apart. During dry weather, the seed is very slow to germinate. I have known it to lie in the ground for six weeks without any perceptible change. To anticipate such a condition, one should mix radish or rape seed with the onion seed in such proportion that one of these seeds will be dropped about every foot. Radish and rape seeds spring up very quickly and are easily seen. This will mark the rows so cultivation can be carried on before the onions are up. If a beating rain occurs before the onions are up, or as they are just appearing, it is liable to smother the young and tender seedlings, but by cultivating after a heavy rain the water draws off rapidly and does less damage. (Of course, this cannot be practiced on strong clay soil.)

It is only in an exceptional year that onions can be grown with profit in this way on weedy land. Keep down all weeds in the middle by the use of a hoe or a wheel-hoe. The weeding, or removing of weeds from the row, is, at best, a slow and expensive task; often the workmen have to get down on their knees and elbows. Only competent laborers should be employed; incompetent ones are liable to disturb the seedlings, or simply pull the tops off the weeds, either of which might go without detection for a week.

CURING THE CROP.

When a majority of the tops fall it is a sign of their being ripe. The crop should be pulled and allowed to dry; this will take about a week of dry weather. If a rain occurs it will be necessary to turn the bulbs, which can be done by using a garden rake with dull teeth, but rain is apt to bleach the crop and so damage the sale. This is best prevented by taking the crop to a curing shed, which simply needs a roof to keep the rain off, and possibly some movable sides for rain-breaks, to prevent a driving rain from beating in.

FIG. 15.

Figure 15 represents a Bermuda onion prepared for crating.

The tops should not be removed until they are dry, when they break easily and can be stripped off without difficulty. (See Fig. 15.) It is usually better to push the crop forward as early as possible. The maturing may be hastened somewhat by knocking the tops over.

As soon as the roots loosen their hold on the ground

ONION. 111

they may be pulled, as there is some danger of their making a second start if the season is rainy. In such a case they must be drawn out and cured quickly. In a dry storing-room onions may be kept for a long time to await a favorable market.

CRATING.

It is not necessary to use a fine material to make onion crates; the poorer quality left from sorting tomato crates will be found to bring as good a price as the finer ones. In packing, the crates should be well filled to prevent the product from being bruised, as they rot down very quickly. All culls should be removed from the field, and composted, to prevent them from drawing insects and growing fungi.

RAISING ONIONS FROM SETS.

The earliest onions to mature in the North are those raised from sets. The operation differs from the above only in that the sets are in a dormant state and are handled more easily. The general directions will remain the same.

VARIETIES.

The only onion that has been mentioned in the previous pages is the Bermuda (see Fig. 15), but it should not be understood that this is the only one worthy of trial.

There are three general classes into which we may divide onions; the Potato onion, the Egyptian onion, and the ordinary Seed onion. The first kind usually does not produce seed, but multiplies by producing small bulblets at the base of the one set out, reminding one somewhat of potatoes in a hill. This is a good kind to produce green onions quickly for bunching.

The Egyptian (see Fig. 16) or perennial tree onion bears the bulblets on the top of a long seed stem while the seed is aborted. These bulblets are set out and produce marketable onions, or they may be pulled for bunching. The third kind to which the Bermuda belongs is usually called the field onion, from the fact that the former kinds are rarely grown extensively, while it is not difficult to find one man growing twenty acres of the last kind.

The Bermuda is the first variety to be mentioned of the last class. It grows to a very large size, and develops early. Its mild flavor and clear white color makes it a favorite on the table. The seed is very high-priced, and much spurious stuff is on the market every year; so we should buy only of reliable seedsmen. From what has been said it should not be understood that all true Bermudas are white as there is also a red kind on the market. The Bermudas have given the best results in our section.

FIG. 16.

Figure 16 represents the Egyptian onion producing sets. Besides the main plant is one of the heads bearing bulblets enlarged.

When the seed is sown late in the fall in northern climates the tops die down while the bulbs are still small. In this way sets of this variety are obtained. These sets may be used in place of seed, but will be found much more expensive, and will probably not pay except for home use.

Large Red Wethersfield is a red-skinned variety that is worthy of trial. It is large, sweet-flavored. The bulb is round and slightly flattened on top.

Yellow Danvers is an excellent variety, grows well from seed; good quality and fair shipper. The bulb is nearly round and of a brownish yellow color.

White Portugal is the leading white variety, and on account of its color, flavor and shape, it usually commands a good price. It is not a good keeper; it will stand marketing, however.

White Multiplier is used largely for pickling. It is highly prized, because of its white color and forming small, plump bulbs. It is reproduced by small offsets or bulbs forming at the base of the one planted.

RESUME.

The onion is a staple vegetable, hence never brings a fancy price, but Southern vegetable-growing will not be on a settled foundation until those engaged in it are prepared to produce crops on narrow margins that will compete with other sections that are as near the market as we are. This crop rarely brings more than two and a half dollars a bushel crate, and often they fall to a dollar a crate. If we can be certain of a profit of ten cents a crate the investment will be a profitable one. Let us calculate the expense of raising an acre by the new culture:

Raising plants..	$ 30
Rent of land.	4
Fertilizer and applying it.	100
Plowing and clearing..	4
Transplanting	40
Seed	5
Cultivating	20
Harvesting	45
Crates, commission and freight	150
	$398

An acre should raise from 400 to 1,000 bushels.

If, then, we are certain of $1.25 a crate for our crop, we will have a net profit of $102. This is 25 per cent. on the money invested for half a year. It is not usual to have to sell the crop for so low a rate, and the estimates given above are liberal in their allowance.

We can say, however, that it will not pay to raise onions for less than $1.00 a crate, under the present conditions of transportation.

LEEK.

This vegetable has not been grown in the South for distant markets, though it stands shipping well. There has not been a demand for it excepting when the Northern markets supplied it. If people know that a certain vegetable is not in the market, they will not demand it, but as soon as this shall be supplied there will be a market for it.

The soil should be a strong loam; if it happens to be a clayey loam, it must have good drainage. Fertilize heavily, and plow thoroughly, but not deeply. Before plowing, all rubbish should have been removed from the ground. Pulverize the soil well, and lay off in rows eighteen inches or two feet apart, and set the plants six inches or a foot apart in the row.

During September, or early in October, prepare a cold frame to receive the seed. Care should be exercised not to allow the soil in the cold frame to become dry, as the seed may fail under such treatment. Keep the weeds down, and if the days become unusually warm, protect the seedlings. When the plants are large enough to handle easily, they should be taken up carefully and transplanted to the field. In taking up leek, it is a good practice to run a spade under the row and lift the plants; then, as the soil separates, they will be removed without injury. If the leaves happen to be long, cut them back a third.

Transplanting may be done during any moist time; usually, watering is not necessary; in other respects, the manipulation of transplanting is like that of onions.

In preparing for market, dig the plants and peel off the outer dry leaves. If the shipment is for a near market, the plants may be washed, but if they will be four or five days in transit, it is not advisable to use water at all. Tie in bunches of six or eight and pack in crates.

The variety known as Large Flag has a strong lead in this country.

FERTILIZER.

The material prepared for onions will make a good fertilizer for this crop. Leek can stand more nitrogenous matter and are slower to grow, hence it is advisable to use more of this element and to use it in a form that will not dissipate readily; such material as barnyard manure and compost are better than the commercial forms. If commercial fertilizers are relied upon, it will be better to make several applicatious. What has been said of the element, nitrogen, is applicable to potash and phosphoric acid.

GARLIC.

Most Americans are strongly averse to the use of this vegetable for flavoring, though it is very highly prized by some European nations. Besides its use as a vegetable, it is largely employed as a medicine. The "seed" is produced as small bulblets, which form at the base of the main bulb, much as in the case of potato onions. It belongs to the same family as onions, and in many respects resembles this vegetable. A rich, heavy soil will be found very excellent for this crop. The demand for it is so limited that we cannot advise it for cultivation on a large scale, but a few square rods or part of an acre may be planted with a reasonable hope of a good return for the labor expended. Prepare the land, and plant the same as in the case of raising onions from sets.

CHIVES.

Most any garden loam will be found suitable for these plants. They are usually propagated from off sets or bulbs that form in the ground, though seed is also produced. This plant is not cultivated to the extent of making a crop, but it is frequently sold in Northern markets as an early spring vegetable. In many families, it takes the place of early green onions. Make the rows about eighteen inches apart and set the plants about two inches in the row.

TOBACCO.

This is one of the non-economic crops; that is, it is a luxury. The world would be quite as well off without it, but people will use it, and others will supply it, so it is our place to consider its culture. There are few, if any plants that are so well understood from a cultural standpoint. The art of raising it is among the most advanced; the fertilizer and its effects on this crop is better understood than for other crops.

VARIETIES.

The varieties are as numerous as the places and districts that grow tobacco for market. For the Lower South, the Veulto Abagio and the Sumatra are doubtless the most profitable for export; and as the seed of the first named is easily obtained, the novice might as well begin and learn on that as on any other.

RAISING THE SEEDLINGS.

The seed is very fine, and very difficult to sow evenly. It is not usually sown by a machine, but this can be used with good results. It is quite usual to sow the seed broadcast in a plant-bed, and then let the plants grow until wanted in the field.

Follow the directions given for the preparation of the cold frame with covering, and you will have a good tobacco-bed. If the season has "gotten ahead of you," a hot-bed may be used with good results. It is a common practice to burn a pile of wood on the plot where the bed is to be; this is for the purpose of killing insects, insect's eggs, weed seed, and to supply some potash and to help irrigation. If the amount of care usually bestowed on a bed of plants be given to a tobacco-bed, no fear need be entertained as to the results. The practice of letting a cold frame grow up to weeds after the plants have been removed is a pernicious practice in any line of vegetable growing. If the seeds are sown in drills, a machine may be used in cultivating and in sowing. Where watering is done by sprinkling from a pot or bucket, the plants are very irregular in growing. In watering a tobaccobed, it should be done thoroughly and at proper times. The bed must not be allowed to become dry after the seed has been sown. Under the proper conditions, the seed produces an abundance of plants even after it is two years old.

It is a common practice to make tobacco beds in a low, moist place; these have had a moderate degree of success, but they are a pioneer method, and must be abandoned for a more certain one if we wish to come out ahead in the competition. It is exceedingly difficult to have enough plants of one size on hand to plant a field by this method of preparing a plant-bed. There seems to be no end of disappointments and failures in the pioneer plant-bed.

If the seed is sown in drills these should be about six inches apart; the plants may be left about one half inch apart or even less in the row. If the seed is sown broadcast, the seedlings should be thinned so they will have about a square inch each. When the cold frame is well made and the protecting cloth is used, it is not necessary to cover the seed, but simply keep the bed moist and covered with a cloth until the plants are quite well developed. This way is rather risky unless one can look after the bed three or four times a day. The protecting cloth is left over the cold frame except during the time of watering. As soon as the little seedlings show a decided green in their seed leaves the protecting cloth can be left off for an hour or so, beginning at sun-rise, if the morning is warm, and again in the evening. Soaking the seed before sowing will hasten germination.

TRANSPLANTING.

Usually the plants need no cultivation in the seedbed, but weeds must be kept down. As the earlier cultivation in the field is somewhat difficult, it is better to have the plants to do as much growing in the plant-bed as possible. They may be left in the plant-bed until the largest leaves are four inches long, if the plants are not so thick as to make them grow spindling.

Transplanting is still done, largely by hand, though several good machines have been invented, and are being used by some.

FERTILIZER FORMULA.

Nitrogen .... 4 per cent.
Potash................................. 10 per cent.
Available phosphoric acid.. 6 per cent.

Use 1,000 to 1,500 pounds of the above formula per acre.

Ordinary manure is not adapted for fertilizers for this crop, and should not be applied unless some other crop is first to be raised. Nor should a commercial fertilizer that contains any chlorin be used, as it produces a tobacco that does not burn evenly.

The following substances can be recommended as free from objectionable qualities:

Element.	Amount of different materials for one acre.
Nitrogen	650 to 1,000 lbs. cotton-seed meal; or 250 to 400 lbs. nitrate of soda; or 400 to 600 dried blood; or 200 to 300 sulphate of ammonia.
Potash	700 to 1,000 lbs. cotton-seed hull ashes. 300 to 500 lbs. saw palmetto ashes; or 200 to 300 lbs. high-grade sulphate of potash.
Phosphoric acid	600 to 900 lbs. acid phosphate; 500 to 750 lbs. dissolved bone.

PREPARATION OF THE LAND.

The land must be deeply and thoroughly prepared. All rubbish must be removed from the field, as any break or hole in the leaf grows larger as the leaf increases in size.

A rich sandy loam that is warm will be found best for this crop. Tobacco can stand a greater drouth than the ordinary field crops. It is always well to send the crop along as rapidly as possible, and to get it in early; by so doing a great deal of the insect ravages will be avoided. The rich alluvial bottoms, or other heavy land, should be avoided, unless one desires to raise coarse and cheap tobacco. Fancy, high priced tobacco, cannot be raised on such land.

The rows are put from four to six feet apart and the plants from a foot to eighteen inches in the row. It takes two or three days to set out an acre by hand, so one cannot wait for a rain, but the plants must be watered, not only once, but several times, during a dry spell before they will have formed a new root system.

CULTIVATION.

There is very little if any tobacco that is cultivated too deeply or too often, but much that receives too little and too shallow cultivation. As long as the horse can pass between the rows without damaging the leaves cultivation may be continued. When the plants are from six to eight inches high they should be hilled up to keep them from being blown over.

TOPPING AND SUCKERING.

When the plant has developed from six to ten leaves the flowering stalk appears, which is cut or pulled off, so as to leave about seven good leaves; this is known as topping. During the growth of a well fed plant, some of the lateral buds develop into shoots; these must be removed as soon as they can be so the plant will send all its energy into the leaves. Topping and suckering and worming require a great deal of attention, and must not be neglected; they are even more important than thorough cultivation.

CUTTING.

It requires judgment and a good deal of knowledge in manipilating tobacco to know just when the crop is "ripe" Usually the plants are cut off just below the lowest good leaf. Much care is exercised in handling while it is being cut. The plants are cut and laid down smoothly and gently to wilt for an hour or so.

HAULING.

The wagon used in hauling the crop to the curing barn is provided with a rack made especially for that work; it is lined with cloth to protect the leaves from being bruised. The rack is nearly four feet wide above and deeper than the height of the largest plant. In loading, the plants are hung over a lath by the lowest leaf, and this lath is put across the rack.

CURING.

When a load arrives at the curing shed, the crop is handled by the laths. Often these are placed across the beams and allowed to cure just as they were placed in the field. The curing of tobacco is a process that is dependent on the action of certain bacteria; if the tobacco is hung too close it will heat and mold; *i. e.*, the temperature induced by oxidation becomes too high for the bacteria, and reaches the best temperature for the growth of molds, consequently these overwhelm other organisms, and the tobacco molds (rots); if the crop is not placed close enough together, the conditions will not allow even the bacteria to develop, and the crop dries but does not cure.

CURING BARNS.

To keep the atmosphere inside of the barns at the best temperature and proper degree of moisture, various devices have been invented. Cupolas on top and ventilators on the sides of the barns, also fire places are among the accessories used. Formerly it was sufficient to air-dry the weed, but the more esthetic taste is not satisfied by such a process now. It is the first-class product that brings the good returns, hence no manipulation from the beginning to the end can be allowed to go amiss. By repeated trials some good buildings have been constructed for the curing of this product. The most complete and perfect that has been employed is one invented by W. H. Snow, of High Point, North Carolina. In this process the leaves are stripped from the stalks in the field. They are then taken to the barn and strung on wires. The wires before being filled with leaves have been passed through pieces of wood the size of a paling picket. These carriers, as we may call them for convenience, are then placed into a frame that can be hoisted to any height in the barn. The advantages of the Snow method of curing tobacco may be briefly stated as follows:

1. The bottom leaves ripen earlier, so these can be removed first from the stalk, thus giving a longer time to harvest the crop, and the upper leaves ripen more fully.

2. The crop can be stored in a much smaller barn without danger of molding.

3. The product is more uniform in color and quality.

4. As flues are used there is no danger from fire, and the heat is more uniform.

STRIPPING AND SORTING.

When the stalks and all are cured in the barn, the leaves have to be stripped off. They are taken from the stalks and placed in bunches that can be quite easily pressed together by both hands. These bunches are then tied at the petiolar end. At the same time the leaves are separated into classes, depending on the condition in which they are cured and whether there are any worm holes in them or not.

After stripping and tying into bunches, or hands, they are packed away in a moist, or rather a clammy, condition. Care must be taken here as there is some danger of molding and also of insect attacks. The different qualities are packed separately. The cases used are either strong boxes or large hogsheads. When the tobacco is nearly dry enough to break when crushed in the hand it is considered right for packing. For making fine cigars the tobacco is put through a second sweating.

When a case has been filled it is pressed down firmly and left in this condition to sweat; during this process it loses its rank flavor and becomes darker.

To make tobacco-growing profitable, capital and experience are required; it is more complicated than other crops.

PARSLEY.

This plant is so easily grown that no garden need be without, and yet it is rather rare, especially in the southern markets. Its production scarcely reaches the dignity of a crop, though around New York and Chicago, the entire crop would amount to acres. The Germans use both roots and leaves as flavoring, while we, Americans, use only the leaves, and these mainly as a garnishing.

Fig. 17.

Sow the seed closely in rows a foot or eighteen inches apart; cover the seed a half inch or less deep. Be sure to watch the conditions of moisture, so as to apply water before the soil dries out to the seed. A pretty plan and useful one is to sow the seed in a broad border row around a flower bed; this remains green during the severest weather that we may have. For this purpose the seed should be sown about the first of November, or in regions north of the lower Gulf region, about the first of October. As the plants grow larger they should be thinned out so as to have from four to nine plants to the square foot.

Parsley can scarcely be over fertilized by using manure. If commercial fertilizer is used, an abundance of cotton-seed meal should be used to obtain the nitrogen.

The general directions for fertilizing, and amounts given for parsnips will be found useful for this crop.

VARIETIES.

For garnishing, the **Moss Curled** and the **Extra Curled** (see Fig. 17.) will be found most desirable, and doubtless all that will be desired. For marketing, the variety known as **Hamburg**, or **Turnip Rooted**, will be an addition. This variety has a large root, which is used for flavoring.

CRESS.

There are several different kinds of plants that are known by this common name. The one that is called water cress (see Fig. 18) is the greater favorite, especially in our section. The best place for planting water cress is some running stream that has a firm or more or less solid bottom. Such little feeders as are supplied by springs will be found to be the best. A small stream that is subject to floods during rainy weather will not be suitable, as the plants are liable to be washed away. A single spring will prove a sufficient area to supply all the cress that a family will want to use.

The sowing is very simple; it amounts to nothing but dropping the seed in a moist place. The best time for this is during September, October or November. A ten-cent package will yield all the cress that several families will care to use. After a little patch is once established it will continue for a very long time, but sooner or later, from various reasons, it will have to be sown again or replanted. There is no extensive market for this product, and yet there are hundreds of families in our section of the country who would be glad to have it. All that is necessary in preparing it for the table is to see that the branches that have been cut off are thoroughly washed and freed from dirt. It is usually eaten with salt. It is most excellent when prepared as a salad.

FIG. 18.

NASTURTIUM.

This belongs to the class of vegetables that are usually used as condiments. The flowers of this plant are sometimes used for decorative purposes, and the seed imparts a flavor to vegetables with which it is prepared, that is considered by many people very delightful. The most favorable soil for this plant is a rather moist garden loam. Some of the varieties have to be trained to trellises or stakes. Some of them are, however, strong enough to hold the flowers and pods from the ground. Make the rows about two feet apart, and plant the seed from six to twelve inches apart in the row. Keep the soil well stirred, but not deeply, and free from weeds.

GLOBE ARTICHOKE (Cyanara Scolymus). This vegetable should not be confused with the Jerusalem Artichoke, *Helianthus tuberosus*. The edible part is located in the flower bud. The receptacle has been excessively developed by the gardeners so that along with the "choke" (bracts) there is a tender tit-bit for the vegetable epicure. (See figure 19.)

FIG. 19.

The seed may be obtained from some American houses, but it comes from England and France. A variety grown in France, and called the Laon Artichoke, is said to be much superior to the ordinary English varieties. Our soil and climate is much like that of France and Globe Artichokes can, therefore, be grown in the South.

Prepare a good rich soil in the ordinary way to the depth of eight or ten inches. Sow the seed in rows three or four feet apart, and thin the plants to three feet apart in the row. When these artichokes are grown regularly, sets can be obtained. The soil must be rich, moist and well drained. During hot, dry weather it may be necessary to supply water that the plants may become well established. It will take a whole year to develop the plants from seed. The second year a few heads are produced; after this the regular crop will come in. Care must be taken to remove all heads as they become fit, as to allow any to go to seed will degenerate the plant very rapidly. As soon as all the heads have been taken the stem should be cut close to the ground. These heads will stand shipping to distant markets if the crate is not so open as to allow them to wilt.

These plants do not come true from seed—*i. e.*, only a portion of the plants raised from seed are good artichokes, consequently we should get a start from seed and then perpetuate our field from slips of these. In removing suckers from the old plant care should be taken that each one has some roots, else they may fail to grow. All plants in the patch that do not produce good artichokes should be destroyed and slips taken only from the best plants.

In northern portions of the South it will be necessary to protect the field with a deep coat of mulch; this will be found to be of advantage in the southern portion also.

The cultivation should be thorough and deep; the roots strike well downward, so there is little danger of mutilating them.

Use a liberal supply of asparagus fertilizer.

TOMATOES.

The history of tomato growing in the South may be cited as a good illustration of the wonderful effect that transportation has upon the product of a section of the country. Twenty years ago it was thought impossible to raise tomatoes in the South; at present there are many localities in the extreme South in which this is the only marketable crop. More and more attention is being constantly given to having this vegetable in the market all the year round. The crop of the far North is usually cut off by frosts in September or October, while that of the States farther south, as North and South Carolina, is not usually cut off until November or December. During December the crop from South Florida is brought forward to the market, continuing to be shipped in as long as the crop will bear transportation. Under favorable conditions, by the first of May, the crop as far North as Georgia begins to ripen, and is pushed forward to the market, crowding the Florida crop out. There are so many engaged in growing tomatoes that only those who are nearest to the market can grow them profitably.

The very high prices paid for tomatoes a few years ago will not be realized again, but those who are engaged in the business must content themselves with small profits. It is rapidly getting to the conditions when only those who have the best information and equipment at hand will be able to make a fair profit on the money invested in the growing of this vegetable. While the Northern gardeners will continue to grow large quantities in greenhouses, the industry will not reach the immense proportions that it was once thought it would. The gardeners of the North bring all the skill and information that is obtainable, to bear upon their work, while many of the gardeners of the South still work in a haphazard way, consequently we see more failures in the latter locality than in the former.

HOT-BEDS.

For that portion of the South where severe winter frosts occur, and where the temperature goes down to 10 to 14° F., it will be necessary to employ hot-beds. While it will be found profitable to use sash and glass, tomatoes can be carried through a temperature of 14° F. by the use of protecting cloth, as described under the head of hot-beds in the introduction.

The soil of the hot-bed should be a sandy loam; where this is not obtainable, a soil may be prepared for the purpose. Use about one-half strong clay and one-fourth coarse sand, fill in the remainder with vegetable mold. The soil should not contain clay enough to allow it to bake, nor should there be enough sand to allow the water to pass off rapidly and the top to become dry during warm, windy days. If the soil will hold water on its surface for an hour, we can be pretty sure that it contains too much clay, and more sand should be added. If undecomposed manure is used as a source of heat it should be tramped in about ten inches thick, and about three inches of the soil placed on this.

Steam is also used as a means of heating hot beds. The pipes are usually laid lengthwise of the beds from four to eight inches under the ground. Hot water may be used in the same way as steam, and is safer in the hands of ordinary help. Some vegetable growers heat their hot-beds with flues. While these work well in the hands of some people, they cannot be recommended without reservation. While the primitive

TOMATOES. 133

method of using manure is still largely employed, it can be used only near large cities where fresh manure can be obtained in large quantities.

COLD FRAMES.

In preparing the soil for the cold frame, we should follow the directions given for the preparation of the soil in hot-beds. It should, however, be made six inches deep. If the cold frame is set on a clay soil, it will be necessary to trench it about so as to allow the water to drain off rapidly. In the matter of protection and location, the cold frame and hot-bed are very similar.

The cold frame will be found profitable in that portion where the coldest part of the winter does not go below 24° F. If, however, we have an occasional winter that gets colder than this, we can make preparations for it. The plants in the cold frame can be covered with litter or leaves, and the protecting cloth rolled down over this; should the cold weather continue for several days, there will be no danger in leaving the bed in this way.

SEED BEDS.

In the extreme South, where the temperature rarely gets to the freezing point during winter, tomatoes may be planted in a seed bed. There should, however, be some protection against the hot sun and against frosty nights and even cold winds. A warm location should be chosen. If it has not a natural wind break, one may be prepared on the east, north and west sides, leaving the south open. Even where the crop is wanted for late fall shipments, seed beds will be found useful.

FERTILIZER FORMULA.

Nitrogen ....4 per cent.
Potash ....7 per cent.
Available phosphoric acid .... 6 per cent.

Use from 1,000 to 2,000 pounds per acre, depending upon the fertility of the soil and the distance apart that the plants are set. If the soil is rich in humus or nitrogenous matter, a portion of the nitrogen should be withheld, as too much of this element makes tomatoes soft and liable to have hollow places in their interior.

FERTILIZER AMOUNTS.

Elements.	Pounds of different material for one acre.
Nitrogen	700 to 1400 lbs. cotton-seed meal; or 400 to 800 lbs. dried blood; or 275 to 550 lbs. nitrate of soda; or 200 to 400 lbs. sulphate of ammonia.
Potash	900 to 1800 lbs. kainit; or 140 to 280 lbs. muriate of potash; or 140 to 280 lbs. sulphate of potash; or 300 to 600 lbs. sulphate of potash and sulphate of magnesia.
Phosphoric acid	600 to 1200 lbs. acid phosphate; or 500 to 1000 lbs. dissolved bone.

VARIETIES.

For shipping purposes, Beauty, Stone and Perfection are general favorites. Usually, we should choose red or purple tomatoes, and such varieties as will color up evenly and deeply. As the winter crop is sold largely upon its looks, a yellow tomato is always a last choice. There are other varieties, such as Paragon and Aristocrat, that are worthy of trial, and some new ones coming in, but the first three named are standards, and can be relied upon as a crop, and for shippers.

All those that have been advised for shipping may

be planted for home use. In addition to these, we may plant Favorite, Buckeye State, for red ones. A few of the yellow varieties, such as Golden Queen and Golden Ball, may also be found interesting and profitable. There are others that may be raised, and some that will produce immense berries, but these as a rule are not profitable, either for distant or local markets. Those that have been recommended for shipping will also be found good for canning and preserving; also excellent for green pickles.

SEED.

We have a great many seedsmen in this country from whom we can obtain our seed. From the glowing descriptions in the seed catalogues, and the marvelous statements that come to our notice, we are almost led to believe that we will have a crop without work or fertilizer if only we purchase *that* seed. However, we should not let glowing descriptions overcome our better judgment. If the seed of a new variety is offered for sale, and we think it will be profitable in our section, a package of seed and one year's test will go a long way to decide the question. When a vegetable-grower has once found a well-established variety to give excellent success, he should not be in a hurry to discard it for something else that he has not tried. Before trusting our hard-earned money in the hands of strangers, we should be quite sure that these strangers have at least a good reputation. In selecting seedsmen from whom to procure our seed, we should first find out whether they make tomato-growing a specialty, or whether it is merely a secondary matter with them. Whenever possible, we should procure our seed from seedsmen who make a specialty of tomato growing. It is all very good for the seedsman to say that he has to be honest, as his reputation is at stake, and that he would lose much by not treating his customers well; but the customer has his money at stake, and therefore is the one to be most careful in the bargain.

Sow the seed about three-fourths of an inch deep; about two to the inch; in drills about three fourths of an inch apart; cover the seed carefully, smooth the ground off, and moisten the soil thoroughly.

TRANSPLANTING.

Under this head, we will simply include the shifting of plants from one portion of the hot bed or cold frame to another. As soon as the plants have grown to be about an inch high, or by the time they are beginning to crowd one another in the seed-drill, they should be taken up and transplanted. Many people are quite timid about transplanting such small seedlings, but if the operation is carried out carefully, there need not be a loss of one plant in a hundred. It is quite customary to plant seedlings before they show their first leaves; that is, while they are in their seed-leaves. Set the plants about an inch apart in the drills, and the drills about three inches apart. Press the soil firmly about the roots of the seedling, and moisten the ground thoroughly. The seedlings should be protected from the direct sunlight for two or three days after they have been transplanted. During this time they form new roots and become established. As soon as practicable, the ground between the drills should be worked with a narrow hoe or other instrument; this will give the air a chance to get into the soil.

The plants should be transplanted again when they crowd one another in the drill; this time to three inches apart in the drill, and the drills the same distance as before. Ordinarily, the plants are left in this bed until they are wanted for setting out.

Another successful method for propagating tomato-plants is to use two and one half inch, three-inch and four-inch paper flower-pots. The two and one half inch flower-pots are filled with soil from a cold frame, or soil prepared similarly to cold frame soil, and four or five tomato seed dropped in each one of these. The flower-pots may be plunged into soil, and be cared for the same as hot-beds or cold frames. As soon as leaves begin to appear, all the plants but the strongest in each pot should be pinched off and this allowed to grow until the roots begin to strike the pot, when the plants should be shifted to a larger one and the additional space filled with soil similar to what was first used. Before transferring from one pot to another, the soil should be wet down thoroughly, and then the pot held upside down, and, by a slight pressure on the bottom, the whole plant will come out at once. This may then be transferred to the second pot without difficulty. When they have been transferred, they should be moistened down again. The above observation will guide us as to the time to transfer to larger pots. By careful manipulation, it will be possible to bring tomato-plants almost to flowering, and in a vigorous condition, in the four-inch flower-pots.

SOIL AND LOCATION.

The soil should be a warm sandy loam with a gentle slope to the south. While this is not always obtainable, it is very desirable to have at least a general slope in this direction ; the minor elevations and depressions may be neglected. By careful tests it has been proved that soil that has a southern slope will be five or six degrees warmer than that which has a northern slope. For this same reason a clay loam should be avoided, except where the crop is wanted for later market ; in such a case a clay soil will be found well adapted to tomato growing. Another very important point in locating a tomato field is that we should see to having a good wind break to the north, east, and west. A great many cold winds that are not severe enough to freeze will be harmful to the plants. In fact, any temperature below 45 will be found very detrimental to the plants, and this will be all the more so if accompanied by high winds, as these carry the warmth away from the plants and soil very rapidly. It is not an uncommon thing to find that the only tomato plants which survived the cold spell are those that were sheltered from the wind by a dense hammock or grove.

PREPARING THE FIELD.

A sandy loam needs very little preparation before transplanting. In fact, it is usually sufficient to work merely a portion of the soil along where the row is to stand. All dead roots, brush, or debris should be removed so that it will not interfere with later cultivation. A two-horse plow may then be used to open out a double furrow where the row is to stand, and the fertilizer worked in this furrow. A portion of it being scattered in the bottom and some of the soil worked on to this, then apply another portion of the fertilizer and work more soil into the furrow, and so on until all the fertilizer has been used. If the plants are to be put in checks four by four feet, the fertilizer may be applied in these checks. Often a portion of the fertilizer is held back and applied after the plants have begun to set fruit. Careful experiments have indicated that where the soil is more or less retentive, nothing is gained, and, indeed, something is lost by appplying the fertilizer at different times. If the season is quite moist the ground will be ready to receive the plants in a week after fertilizing. If, however, the soil remains unusually dry it may be much longer.

TOMATOES.

SETTING OUT.

Before the plants are set out in the field they should be hardened off, but this must be done quite carefully. It is not a good practice to withhold the moisture all at once, but it should be done gradually. In this way the plants adapt themselves to particular conditions, and are thus much better able to stand the shock which they receive at setting out. A week or ten days before the time the plants are ready to be set in the field, just enough moisture should be applied to keep the plants in the seed bed from becoming wilted. It will be found that by following this from day to day that the plants will be in a much better condition to set out than they were at the time when hardening off was begun.

The distance at which tomatoes should be set varies with the fertility of the field and with the varieties used. If we have an ordinary field that produces about 30 bushels of corn to the acre, and wish to use about 1,000 pounds of fertilizer to the acre, it will be well to plant in checks, four by four feet. If, however, the land is very fertile they may be planted as close as three by three feet, or the rows may be planted four feet apart, and the plants set two feet in the row.

A great many devices for transplanting purposes have been invented, but none seem to meet the demand fully. Some machines are drawn by horse power and others worked by hand. The greatest objection against some of these is the cost of the implement. So, for various reasons, up to the present time the bulk of the crop is still transplanted by hand, and as this is not an especially expensive operation, it will be continued for many years to come. A man or strong boy can set out an acre of tomatoes in a day when they are placed in checks four by four feet. Consequently, it should not cost more than $1 to $2 to set out an acre of tomatoes, including the sets. Various labor saving, or so called short cuts, have also been resorted to by tomato growers. One that has been recommended by several tomato growers is to plow out a furrow with a one-horse plow and drop tomato plants along this furrow at proper intervals. The plants are so dropped that the heads all project to one side of the furrow. A small furrow is then thrown upon their roots, care being exercised not to cover them too far. The plow is then run down the outer side of the row, which will set the plants more or less erect. For such an operation it will be necessary to have plants that are more or less drawn out, and usually considered too large for transplanting. This method is too slip shod for ordinary success, but some portions of it may be used to advantage.

A handy setting-out tray may be made very cheaply by using an ordinary soap box that is six inches deep, twelve or fourteen inches wide, and ten inches long. One end of this is knocked out and a bale fastened from one side to the other. The plants may be carried in this to the field, and, as they are wanted, taken out of the open end to place in position.

CULTIVATING.

This work is simple and not laborious. While most of it is performed by a one horse plow, much time and labor could be saved by using a two-horse plow; this cannot be used to advantage in fields that contain many stumps. The ordinary two horse corn plows that are used by the farmers of the West could be used with profit. As soon as the tomatoes begin to show bloom or set fruit much care should be taken not to disturb the roots, as this is liable to shock the plants and cause the blooms to fall.

PRUNING.

There is, probably, no other vegetable in cultivation that has received as much attention as tomatoes, although it is one of the last that has been introduced. There are two reasons for pruning tomatoes. The first is to bring the earliest fruit in earlier than would be done without pruning. The second, is to develop the fruit to its fullest extent. The earliest form of pruning was to remove all the side shoots, and then train the plant up to the main stem, or vine, as it is usually called; this being either tied to a stake or fastened to a trellis. While this does much toward producing a good crop, it does very little in the way of bringing the crop in earlier. From experience, it has been proven that the earliest tomatoes can be forced to ripen a week or even two weeks earlier than where the tomatoes have not been topped. By topping or cutting out the terminal bud at just below the second cluster of blossom, before the first cluster has begun to open, the growing force is thrown into the first cluster. It is not at all uncommon, under such treatment, to have this cluster produce from five to seven berries, and all of these ripen at nearly the same time. While the crop is much smaller than it would have been as a whole, if no topping had occurred, the earlier crop comes in so much earlier that it more than compensates for the loss in quantity.

Pruning should not be carried too far, however, as the leaf surface of the plant must be sufficient to assimilate the crude material that is absorbed by the roots. If the leaf surface is too small, so much absorbed matter will be sent to them that the tissues and cells become swollen and unable to perform their functions. It should always be kept in mind that we want to check further growth of the stem and further forma-

142   VEGETABLE GROWING.

tion of fruit, but not interfere with the production of leaf surface, so the mere removing of buds and flower clusters will be the pruning desired. The extent to which pruning can be carried will depend largely upon the variety, condition of weather, and kind of land. A dwarf variety, during dry weather and on poor, dry soil, can be pruned much more severely than a large-growing variety, during rainy season, on fertile land; in fact, the latter will scarcely permit any pruning.

STAKING.

The usual varieties of tomatoes that are grown for Northern markets have not a strong enough stem to carry the weight of the leaves and fruit, consequently they fall over and the fruit comes in contact with the soil; this renders it unsightly and also quite accessible to attack from insects and fungi. Consequently a great many tomatoes are lost when the vines are not staked and tied. Stakes used for this purpose are about one and one-half inches square and three feet long. One of these is driven down by each tomato plant and the plant tied firmly to this. Some strong wrapping cord, that is at the same time quite soft, is employed. The cord should be wrapped twice around the stake at the proper height and then a hard knot tied. Then pass the string around the tomato plant and tie the knot so as to hold the plant loosely. The double wrap around the stake secures the cord from slipping up and down, while the cord tied loosely about the plant prevents any binding or cutting. Staking and tying tomatoes will not be found profitable where land is cheap and labor dear.

TRELLISING.

The trellising of tomatoes is carried on very largely in portions of the United States where tomatoes are selling at quite a low figure, and yet it is found profitable to do this work. In preparing the trellis, posts are placed in the ground at proper distances and wire attached to these, much as the vineyardists do in their vineyards. The tomatoes are then tied to the wire, or if the wires have been placed close enough together, the plants are simply trained to them. Ofttimes a lath is placed down where the tomato plant is standing to guide it more or less in the proper direction.

Either staking or trellising should be practiced in the South, where a late summer or early fall crop is wanted for home use.

PICKING.

This is the busiest season of the year for the tomato-grower. If his crop is ready to go forward, it must be put on the market without any delay. The loss of twenty-four hours will often work a damage of $100 or more on a single car-load; consequently everything should be in readiness and all the necessary hands ready to go at the work in business fashion. During the cool winter months the tomatoes must be allowed to take on even a slight tinge of red before picking, otherwise they will arrive in the market too green. During the warm summer months these same tomatoes would have arrived in the market over-ripe; therefore, we must allow the tomatoes to become riper on the vines during cold weather than in the warm portion of the year. In the warm spring months, it is sufficient to allow the tomatoes to become full grown and a slight change from green to a whitish color, but in this matter it will require considerable experience before one is able to pick just at the right time.

The picking is usually done in ordinary market baskets. Hands for this purpose must be selected with some degree of caution, as only those who can discriminate quite well and who are not rough with the vegetables should be employed. At convenient places in the field boxes are placed; these boxes are about ten inches wide, fourteen deep, and thirty long; they hold about two crates. In making such boxes it will be found best not to leave any cracks open and to make them of whole boards; this lessens the danger of injuring the fruit. Strips are nailed across the ends, which serve as handles and at the same time give additional strength to the box. It is quite desirable to make the box large enough to hold about two crates, as this weight usually requires the attention of the person handling it, and there will be less danger of carelessness.

PACKING HOUSE.

It is very desirable to have the packing house located at a depot or railway switch, so the crated vegetables can be loaded directly on the car; this will save one handling, and consequently compensate for a considerable haul. If, however, the packing house is so far that the fruit must be handled, it should then be placed as near the center of the field as possible. There are a good many reasons why a packing house should not be near dwellings.

The interior of the packing house should be arranged so that the boxes are received from the wagon and set on the floor without any high lifting; they should be on a level with the sorter's bench. As any lifting is an absolute loss, we can see the force of the argument that the packing house be planned carefully. After the tomatoes are received, they should be sorted immediately and the different kinds placed in separate places to be packed. The person placed at the sorter's bench must be quick at discriminating and active with his hands. Chutes can be arranged to carry the fruit to the different tables, or it can be made to run into different boxes, which when full may be put in place for wrappers. The wrapper's bench should not be higher than the boxes that receive the fruit from the sorters. After the fruit has been packed it should be continued to be carried downward, but in no case should there be any lifted upward. The packed fruit may then be delivered to the other side of the packing house and carted to the station.

SORTING.

The successful tomato growers usually sort their tomatoes in various grades, depending very largely upon the tastes of the grower and the market for which they are prepared. There are two general grades that are recognized by all tomato growers, and they are usually observed even by persons who make no pretence of grading their tomatoes; these are usually spoken of as "Ripes" and "Greens." These two grades give the grower a chance to distribute the fruit to different markets and have them all arrive there in suitable condition. More advanced tomato growers make, besides these, other divisions, as "large ripes," "small ripes," large greens," and "small greens." While it seems like a great deal of work to separate the fruit into grades, it is found to be very profitable. The large, well formed tomatoes are then wrapped in different kinds of paper to suit the grower and packed in carriers, while the small ones are simply packed in crates. There are two advantages in packing the large tomatoes in carriers; first, they sell better; second, it takes fewer tomatoes to fill a crate, while the selling price remains the same. In sorting the fruit in various sizes or grades, one will be better able to meet the desires of different markets and the different desires of the same market.

Very few tomato growers pay any attention to local or near-by markets, so it not unfrequently happens that tomatoes are being shipped to New York at a loss, when our southern towns and cities have to depend on northern canned goods. Many instances of this kind could be cited without going back more than a year.

The usual tomato crate holds about twenty-four quarts, and should be made of first-grade material; no pains should be spared to make the crate and the material in the crate look as attractive as possible. It is found profitable to even go as far as to use a tinge of color on the lid of the crate, and represent a highly-colored tomato, as a trade mark.

SUMMER AND FALL CROP.

While many of our neighbors vigorously declare that tomatoes cannot be grown during the summer and fall in the South, we can content ourselves by saying that many people are not only able to raise them, but sell them with profit. It will, doubtless, only be a few years until it will be as easy to raise a crop of tomatoes in the summer or fall as it is in the spring. Many of us can remember the time when it was generally reported that tomatoes could not be raised at all in the South.

In preparing for fall crop, a cold frame should be prepared, as for the spring crop. The protecting cloth in this case is used for an entirely different purpose, however. At this time of the year we want it to keep the sun off and the rain out.

All the watering had better be done by hand. In setting the tomatoes out, care should be taken to provide for them a shelter by using slats, or plant them in a pine forest. If one intends to build a shade of slats, this can be easily done by placing stringers on the tops of seven foot posts, and then laying slats across these stringers, leaving as much space between the slats as the width of one of them. This will keep out one-half of the sunshine, and will modify the temperature so as to allow the tomato to grow vigorously. Late in the fall frosts are liable to occur, and these same shades will protect the plants from frosts as they do from the sun in summer.

SAVING SEED.

The seed that is offered on the general market is so excellent and so cheap that it scarcely seems worth the while to save any, but we shall never have varieties that are better adapted to our conditions than we have now, until we have some seed grower who will select the tomatoes with our special wants in view. There are several points of difference between tomatoes growing in the South and in the North, and such conditions as are not taken into consideration by seed growers of the North. Consequently, we should, at least make an attempt at saving our own seed. Select the very best plants from the variety that has always done well and allow these to ripen their fruit; this may then be gathered and broken into pumice, or it may be cut open and the seed, together with the parts that contain the seed, taken out and placed in a barrel to macerate for a day or so. In the meantime it should be stirred to keep it as homogeneous as possible. To separate the seed from the pumice, follow the directions given under egg-plant.

CANNING.

This subject is frequently discussed in connection with vegetable growing. While a great many people think that it would be highly profitable to start a canning factory, we have very few Southern canneries that are in successful operation to-day. There are various causes operating against the erection and running of a canning factory. The greatest difficulty is the uncertainty of having material to work up when the season comes. During good vegetable seasons the crop is exhausted by the end of the shipping season, consequently no factory could afford to buy the vegetables in competition with the northern markets. It is also true that the factory would be operated for a small portion of the year, possibly for three or four months. As soon as we perfect vegetable or fruit growing to such a degree as to have ripe material coming in for canning, during eight or ten months of the year, there will be plenty of capital to invest in factories.

Under present conditions it might be quite possible that the different communities could establish factories on a co operative basis. This is done in a dairying section, and also in some fruit growing sections of the United States. Such a corporation does business just as if it were a private enterprise. The advantage in this plan is that many are working for a common cause. The expense of erecting a canning factory is by no means the most important consideration. An establishment that would cost from $500 to $1,000 would be able to do the work that would be required of it for a very large tomato-growing district.

The operation of canning is exceedingly simple, yet it requires an expert to do the work well, and to know that when it is done the material will not degenerate in the cans. The principle involved is simply this: The material to be canned is placed under a temperature sufficient to kill all living organisms contained therein, and in this condition it is sealed. Under these circumstances there can be no degenerating material that has been canned, no fermenting, no rotting, and the canning master who can accomplish this and not destroy the special flavor of tomatoes is successful.

For home use tomatoes may be canned as easily as other material. The fruit is brought in, pared or otherwise prepared, as for the table, and then subjected to heat not quite to the boiling point, but just at the verge. They are then kept in this condition for an hour or two, and while in this heated condition transferred to the jars. These jars, their covers, and all connected with them, should previously have been subjected to a temperature at least equal to boiling water. It is not sufficient to rinse them in hot water, or merely to scald them, but they should be kept in boiling water for several minutes, or even half an hour, then, immediately, without allowing to cool, the hot tomatoes are transferred to the cans, which are immediately sealed, air tight. If these precautions are observed to a letter, it will be found that a very small per cent., if any, of the fruits will spoil if they are kept for a year or more. As stated before, the principle in canning is simply this: We must kill off all living organisms in the cans; all living organisms in the fruit, and then fill the cans with tomatoes, close them up without introducing any of these organisms. As fermentation and decay are omnipresent, falling into everything that is left open for a minute, we will see that it is necessary to keep the temperature high enough to kill them, up to the very minute our material is canned, and then keep it from being opened again. It is immaterial whether the fruit is sweetened at the time the canning is done or not. The keeping qualities will still be the same.

EGG-PLANT.

This vegetable is rapidly becoming a money crop for the South ; although it can be grown in gardens of the North, it does not flourish to such an extent as it does in the South. The greatest obstacle in the way of success for this crop is that the gardeners rarely ever supply enough fertilizer to the soil. A successful grower in Florida began by raising ten acres, but did not make a profit on the crop; he then reduced his acreage to five, and used the same amount of fertilizer that he put on the ten acres before. Later,

FIG. 20.

he again cut down the acreage to two and one-half acres, but kept the amount of fertilizer at the original figure, and also bestowed as much attention to the two and one half acres as he did formerly on the ten acres. The two and one-half acres then gave him more fruit of a better quality, and a better size, than on the original ten acres, and at the same time the field became profitable. This instance illustrates a point that has been insisted upon before; that is, we should resort to intensive, rather than extensive vegetable growing.

EGG-PLANT.

VARIETIES.

The early varieties are not usually so productive as later ones. The New York Improved Spineless will mature several weeks later than the Black Pekin, but the later is much more productive. The New York Purple and Black Pekin are excellent varieties for shipping or for home use, but the New York Spineless and Early Long Purple make earlier vegetables.

HOT BEDS AND COLD FRAMES.

For early fruit, and the northern parts of this section, it will be necessary to use a hot bed and later a cold frame. The hot bed properly prepared will save these plants through frosts of 14° F. Of course such extreme cold is by no means healthful to the plant, but the plants may be saved from destruction. For egg-plant seedlings, make the manure in the hot bed about a foot thick, and bank up the outside of the frame to the rim. Use two sheets of protecting cloth, with some space between them; cover the outer edges to keep the wind from getting under them. During cold weather, the plants will make very little progress, however, but the gentle bottom heat causes them to make a good root system.

As soon as all danger from further frosts is past, the seedlings may then be thinned out; and if any thin places occur, these may be filled in with seedlings from places where the plants are too thick in the row. The plants should have about an inch in the row, and the row about three inches apart. As soon as the plants begin to crowd one another, they should be transplanted to another frame; this time each plant should be given about two inches in the row, and the rows four inches apart. Inexperienced people are somewhat timid in removing egg-plant seedlings, or transplanting them, because they fear they will be injured in the operation; but experience has taught us that they may be removed, or re-set, when small, without any disadvantage to the plant. The time to sow the seed depends upon the time when the last killing frost occurs in our section.

The seed may be sown in cold frames in warm sections, but the plants will not come along so rapidly as they would in a hot bed. They will, however, mature very much earlier than the Northern grown product, and consequently be marketable when the prices are still very good. The same precautions for hot-beds should be observed for cold frames.

USING FLOWER POTS.

Egg-plant seedlings are somewhat sensitive about having their roots disturbed, consequently some gardeners have used several sizes of flower-pots to prevent this injury; for this operation they secure paper flower-pots of various sizes, beginning usually with two and one-half inch ones. These cost about $2.50 per thousand. The pots are filled about four-fifths full of potting soil, to which has been added a liberal supply of fertilizer prepared for egg-plant. Six or eight seed are dropped in each one of these, and the pots are then placed in the hot bed or cold frame, as the gardener desires. Some plunge the pots into the soil, while others do not; the former way requires less attention, but destroys the pots in one year. The seedlings grow in these pots just as though they were in the hot bed, but from time to time the gardener examines the plants to see that they do not become pot-bound, or do not send their roots through the bottom of the pot. As soon as either of these occur, the plants are shifted to a larger sized pot, which is usually a three-inch one. The increased space is filled up with soil similar to that formerly used, and the pots are then placed where the other size stood; of course they require more room. As soon as the fertilizer in the three-inch pots has been pretty well appropriated by the plants, they are then transferred to a larger sized, say four-inch; some prefer six inch pots. The treatment in each of these pots is similar to that given in the first. It should have been mentioned, however, that before shifting the plants from the smallest pot to the larger that the smaller plants should be pinched off, leaving one plant in the pot. Under proper manipulation, plants may grow to bearing-size in six-inch pots, but this is not profitable in our section. Plants should not be removed to the field until the soil is warm and all danger of cold spells is past.

In using flower pots for propagating egg plants great care must be taken that at no time the plants become checked in their growth, as this will materially reduce their productive properties, and consequently prove a serious disadvantage, There are are two points always to be borne in view—first, that fresh·fertilizer is applied as soon as the earlier supply has been used; second, plants should not become potbound. Under proper manipulation plants may be grown in three-inch pots, from which marketable fruit can be obtained in sixty days after setting out.

SOIL AND PREPARATION.

This plant requires good rich loam that is very deep. It is a deep feeder, consequently it cannot stand moist or soggy land. The plowing should be deep and thorough. Any refuse material or debris, also decaying vegetable matter, should be removed from the field.

Lay the field off in rows four feet apart, and set the plants from two to four feet apart in the row, depending upon the variety and fertility of the soil. In setting plants in the field they should be placed an inch or so below the level of what they stood in the hotbed or cold frame.

FERTILIZER FORMULA.

Nitrogen........................4 per cent.
Potash..........................9 per cent.
Available phosphoric acid....5 per cent.

Use 1,500 to 2,500 pounds per acre of the above formula. This plant is one of the most sensitive to improper use of fertilizer that we have, shedding its fruit or failing to set it at all if badly prepared. Consequently, we have a great many cases of failure, and it is very difficult for the "plant doctor" to tell what ails the plant, as the symptoms of many ailments are so similar that they cannot be distinguished. A very successful way of applying the fertilizer is to make a double furrow where the row is to be. Apply a portion of the fertilizer down the row and then mix in a portion of the soil that has to be thrown out, then apply more of the fertilizer and work in more soil. Continue this until the fertilizer has been deposited evenly throughout the entire furrow. If the plants are to be set in checks 4x4 feet, it will be sufficient to fertilize the ground for about a foot on each side of the check.

The following table of fertilizers will give the desired amounts of each element per acre:

EGG-PLANT.

Element.	Pounds of different material for one acre.
Nitrogen	1000 to 1600 lbs. cotton seed meal; or 600 to 1000 lbs. dried blood; or 400 to 650 lbs. nitrate of soda; or 325 to 525 lbs. sulphate of ammonia.
Potash	1600 to 2000 lbs. kainit; or 275 to 450 lbs. muriate of potash: or 275 to 450 lbs. sulphate of potash; or 500 to 800 lbs. sulphate of potash and sulphate of magnesia.
Phosphoric acid	750 to 1200 lbs. acid phosphate, or 600 to 1000 lbs. dissolved bone.

CULTIVATION.

The field cultivation of this plant is very simple. The soil should be stirred deeply and well. The cultivation should not be carried to the extent of tearing the roots, however. Those who are not acquainted with the root system of this plant will find it profitable to dig into the soil frequently and find out how near the top and how far the roots extend. During rainy weather it will be necessary to plow the field as often as twice a week. This cannot, of course, be done when the field is on strong clay soil. During dry weather plowing will not have to be repeated so often nor so deeply, but merely stirring the upper stratum to the depth of three or four inches will be sufficient.

GATHERING.

It is quite important that we be able to tell just when the fruit is ready for market. While the early crop brings the best price, usually, the fruit is liable to be too small and green for the market. Fruit that is too ripe is quite worthless. As soon as the berry turns from a lustrous purple to a dull color, you may suspect that shipping time has arrived. The best way is to test a few eggs by cutting through the center; if the seeds are well formed, the time for gathering has arrived. They should not be allowed to remain on the plant, however, until the seed coat begins to harden. In case of Black Pekin or Improved New York Purple the fruits are about seven inches long. Cut the fruit with a stem about three-fourths of an inch long.

MARKETING.

This vegetable is usually marketed in barrels, but the variation in the size of barrels, and the fact that much of the fruit is not open to inspection makes this less desirable than crates would be. As the demand for this crop increases it will be necessary to abandon this primitive way of marketing the crop. A crate of uniform size is very desirable, but it should be made large enough to hold about as much as a barrel. Under such conditions we could still continue to quote egg plant by the barrel, and at the same time know very definitely how much there was in one of the crates. Under the present conditions the honest vegetable grower is imposed upon by the sharp commission merchant, as all barrels are quoted at the same price. A lot of small barrels will be quoted much lower, and the vegetable grower will interpret that as a fall in the price of egg plants.

SEED SAVING.

Considerable time elapses between the marketing time and the ripening of the seed. Usually the fruit intended for seed may be left on the plants until they decay, but this is not necessary, as the seed can be gathered and saved for planting as soon as it becomes meaty. Gather the fruit as for shipping, and take them to the packing house. Here they may be left for several days or for a week if the pile is not too large. When a considerable lot is on hand a time may be set aside for taking the seed out. By examin-

EGG-PLANT. 157

ing the fruit it will be noticed that about one-third of the meat may be cut away from the stem end without harming the seed. Pare this away, remove all the skin, and quarter it with a dull knife. If rollers of an old cane mill are at hand they may be set far enough apart in blocks, to crush the fleshy portion without injuring the seed. If one has an acre or so from which to save seed, it will pay to construct a set of wooden rollers in absence of cane mill rollers. Put this crushed material in a barrel for maceration; do not make the barrel more than two-thirds full of pumice and water. Set the barrel out of the hot sun, but keep it in some warm place. In twenty-four hours stir the pumice up thoroughly, so as to have all parts mixed evenly. The pumice may be left to ferment for two or three days, depending upon the temperature in the meantime. Secure a No. 3 sieve that will go handily into the inside of the barrel. Fill a half barrel with water and place a sieve in the water, but not on the bottom of the half barrel. The sieve may be held in place by wires stretched across the barrel. Dip the seed out of the barrel and put them into the sieve, work the pumice around so as to break it into small pieces. Some of the pumice and the seed will go through the sieve and fall to the bottom, while the larger portions will be taken out and thrown away, then a fresh lot will be taken from the barrel and the work continued as before until three or four inches of material has collected in the bottom of the barrel. This may be turned out into a barrel and a second sieve of No. 6 wire used for the second preparation. The meshes of this sieve are just large enough to let all the seed pass through and screen out all the pumice that is left. As soon as all the seed has been worked through the second sieve, it may be placed on a third sieve, with No. 12 wire mesh. This sieve permits all fine pumice to get through and screens out all seed. As soon as a large quantity has collected in the sieve it may be put aside for an hour or so to drain, then spread out on canvas, or other suitable place to dry, but this should not be done in the hot sun, as the high temperature is liable to injure its vitality. The seed should be dried as quickly as possible, as there is danger of its beginning to sprout. If the fruit has been allowed to decay or the pumice allowed to remain in the barrel for several days there is danger of the seed germinating during this time. When the seed has been thoroughly dried, it should be winnowed or run through a fanning mill to get rid of all chaff. Tie the seed up in suitable packages and place where it is safe from attacks of mice or roaches. It is preferable to tie the seed in parchment or glazed paper to keep it from getting moist. In this way seed may be kept for two or three years without losing its vitality.

PEPPERS.

This is becoming one of the vegetables for which there is a steady demand during the winter months. While shipments of large size cannot be disposed of very well, the demand is above the supply. Most of the product for the northern and eastern markets come from the Bermudas, Bahamas and Cuba. The crop is not grown to any extent in the Lower South. The main reason it is not more extensively cultivated is the same as that given for the neglect of the egg-plant.

It is not advisable to plant a large field to peppers, but vegetable-growers should have about an acre to ship in connection with other early vegetables.

Fig. 21.

VARIETIES.

Among the large sweet varieties we have the Large Bell, or Bull Nose, (see Fig. 21), and another good variety is the County Fair. The first named and those that grow similarly are to be preferred for shipping purposes. The County Fair has several advantages, however, for the home use and the local market. Among the hot varieties we have the Small Chili (see Fig. 22). The Celestial is also excellent, besides being highly remunerative. If one desires to raise hot varieties for market, Small Chili is probably best.

Fig. 22.

HOT-BEDS AND COLD FRAMES.

For the upper portion of the Lower South it will be necessary to provide hot-beds to grow this vegetable, but in the lower portions where frosts do not occur, or only occasionally, cold frames will be sufficient. If one is located in a clay country, he should take about one-fourth clay, one-half vegetable mold and one-fourth coarse sand. To this add the necessary fertilizer to make the soil of the hot-bed or cold frame. The soil of the hot-bed may be tested by wetting it down thoroughly and returning in two or three hours; if the soil can be squeezed into a more or less solid mass, there is not enough sand and too much clay in the mixture. If, however, the mass does not remain in a body but breaks up readily, the soil will be about right. On the other hand, if the water drains off immediately, and the soil becomes dry to the depth of one-half inch in the course of four or five hours, in the sunshine or gentle wind, too much sand has been used and a little more clay should be introduced. Make the rows about three inches apart and drop the seed about three to the inch. Cover the seed to the depth of about three-fourths of an inch. Before the seedlings begin to crowd one another they should be transplanted, and this time about an inch in the row and the rows three inches apart. Before they begin to be spindling in this bed they should be transferred to another bed, this time planting the seedlings three by three inches.

A very successful and handy way is to make use of two and one-half, three-inch and four-inch flower-pots in their respective orders. When these flower-pots are used the soil should be the same as in hot-beds without flower pots.

The seed should be sown from 40 to 60 days before the average time of the last frost. The rapidity with which the seedlings come along will depend upon the amount of sunshine and warm weather, and also upon the attention of the gardener, consequently the statement as to the time required for the seedlings to grow to planting out size cannot be made definitely.

SOIL AND PREPARATION.

A warm sandy loam that retains moisture in the subsoil will be found very excellent. In preparing land for peppers care should be taken to remove all decaying matter and rubbish from the field. This does no damage in some sections where gardening is carried on extensively, but in the Lower South it should be avoided.

Lay the rows off two or two and one-half feet apart

and set the plants from one to one and one half feet apart in the row. The variation in the distances in which they are planted should depend on the conditions of the land and varieties which are being fruited. The larger or sweet varieties require more room than the small hot ones.

CULTIVATION.

Cultivation should be carried on thoroughly and deeply, but should never be carried to the extent of injuring or destroying the roots of the plants. This, of course, must be ascertained by observation. An easy and satisfactory way is to remove the soil from beside a thrifty plant and follow the roots to the end. After the plants have reached their bearing size, it is well to discontinue the deep plowing, but to continue the cultivation of the upper stratum of the soil, until shipping season is over. When the plants are no longer wanted, they should be destoyed at once; especially should this be done if another crop of peppers is to be grown on this land the following year.

MARKETING.

As soon as the large varieties have reached the size of two inches in diameter, they are usually considered right for marketing, but one must be guided by experience in the matter. The earliest shipments are usually the most remunerative, so we want to hurry the first of it to the market.

In removing the fruit from the plant, it should never be torn off, but a knife or scissors should be used. In cutting, the stem should be left about an inch long, so as to prevent excessive loss of moisture.

It is not necessary usually to wait for the fruit to become slightly wilted before packing, but sometimes this may be done to advantage. The fruit is packed

PEPPERS. 163

in the usual vegetable crate, with the top pressed down firmly, to prevent the fruit from shaking about.

SAVING SEED.

After shipping season is over, it may be to one's advantage to save his own seed, or to sell to his neighbors. The matter of saving seed is very simple and easy. The fruit is allowed to become ripe, then picked, allowed to dry, and the seed removed. It will be necessary to protect this from mice, rats, or other vermin. Under ordinary circumstances, the seeds will retain their vitality for a number of years.

FERTILIZER FORMULA.

Nitrogen .... 4 per cent.
Potash .... 9 per cent.
Available phosphoric acid ... 5 per cent.

Use 750 to 1,250 pounds per acre of the above formula. Use the same precautions in applying the material as directed per egg-plant.

The following table will give the desired amounts per acre of each fertilizer element:

Element.	Pounds of different material for one acre.
Nitrogen	500 to 800 lbs. cotton-feed meal; or
	300 to 500 lbs. dried blood; or
	200 to 325 lbs. nitrate of soda; or
	160 to 250 lbs. sulphate of ammonia.
Potash	800 to 1,000 lbs. kainit; or
	150 to 225 lbs. muriate of potash; or
	150 to 225 lbs. sulphate of potash; or
	250 to 400 lbs. sulphate of potash and sulphate of magnesia.
Phosphoric acid....	400 to 600 lbs. acid phosphate; or
	300 to 500 lbs. dissolved bone.

It seems that no chemical analysis has thus far been made of this vegetable, so we have no definite information as to the amounts of the different fertilizer elements that are removed from the soil. The foregoing table and formula can be only approximately correct.

OKRA.

This vegetable is also called gumbo. Its desirable qualities lie in the muscilage of the pods. The taste for this is more or less an acquired one, however; when used in small quantities in soups, only a very few people object to it. Besides its use in soup, it may be pickled and also prepared as a dish by itself.

Any good cotton land will produce okra, and, like cotton, it is partial to a warm sandy loam. For shipping purposes, a warm sandy loam should be chosen, and this highly fertilized, unless it is already rich. Okra grown on poor soil is stringy and wanting in muscilage.

Prepare the land thoroughly and deeply. The roots of this plant descend below any ordinary plowing, so the plant can stand an unusual drouth without apparently suffering.

Fig. 23.

VARIETIES.

The larger varieties are not so profitable nor so desirable as the smaller or dwarf. Little Gem and White Velvet are among the favorite dwarf varieties. Improved Green is a good medium-sized variety. (See Fig. 23.)

Make the rows two and a half or three feet apart and drop a seed about every three inches. When the plants are about six inches high, thin to a foot in the row for dwarf varieties, and to about one and a half feet for the half dwarf varieties. If the large varieties are planted, the rows may be made four feet apart and the plants thinned out to two feet in the row. Plant the seed an inch deep.

The cultivation should be deep and thorough. The plants are so strong that there is rarely any occasion for the use of a hoe, but the work may all be done with a plow.

In gathering for a distant market, cut the stems on the pods an inch or so long to prevent wilting. Figure 23 shows some of the pods cut in the proper way.

Ship in an ordinary vegetable crate. Pack down firmly, so the product will not shake about on the way. There is very little demand for this vegetable in the markets of the Northwest, so we must ship to some near-by market or to the East.

The seed is easily saved. When the pods are ripe, remove from the plant—they break easily, and the seed comes out readily.

FERTLIZER FORMULA.

Nitrogen ....4 per cent.
Potash..................................4 per cent.
Available phosphoric acid .... 8 per cent.

Use 1000 to 1500 pounds of the above formula to the acre. Land rich in vegetable matter will require less nitrogen.

FERTILIZER AMOUNTS.

The following table gives the amounts of different

materials required to give the desired amount of each element:

Elements.   *Pounds of different material for one acre.*

Nitrogen
- 700 to 1000 lbs. cotton-seed meal; or
- 400 to 600 lbs. dried blood; or
- 275 to 400 lbs. nitrate of soda; or
- 200 to 300 lbs. sulphate of ammonia.

Potash
- 500 to 750 lbs. kainit; or
- 80 to 120 lbs. muriate of potash; or
- 80 to 120 lbs. sulphate of potash; or
- 175 to 250 lbs. sulphate of potash and sulphate of magnesia.

Phosphoric acid
- 800 to 1200 lbs. acid phosphate; or
- 700 to 1000 lbs. dissolved bone.

CUCUMBERS.

This has become one of the leading vegetables for the Lower South. It stands shipping to distant markets remarkably well. In that portion of this district where killing frosts occur, the seedlings should be started in a cold-frame or in a hot-bed. This seems like very remarkable advice to those who have tried to transplant them, but it is easy enough when you know how. For every acre to be planted, procure twelve hundred two inch paper flower pots; the same number of four-inch, and if very early "cukes" are wanted, the same number of six-inch. Use only the best seed, and plant four in each pot. These pots should be filled to within a half inch of the top, with good potting soil; this should be done six weeks earlier than the last frost usually occurs, if it is intended to use only the two smaller sized pots; but about nine weeks, if the three sizes are to be used. The cost of the pots in the former case will be less than nine dollars; in the latter, about twenty-five dollars. There is no doubt but that one could obtain a liberal discount on these pots, if a large quantity were bought at one time. If these pots are not sunk into the sand, they will stand for two crops. During their growth, the plants should be examined frequently to see that they do not become pot-bound. They should be shifted to a large pot as soon as the soil is permeated by the roots. This may be tested by removing the soil from one of the pots, which may be done easily as follows: Hold a pot upside down, press on the bottom—this will loosen the soil; the condition of the roots can now be examined without difficulty. As soon as the roots have taken up most of the space in the pot, shift the plant to a larger one.

If the plants show any signs of yellowing, they may be restored to health by a light application of liquor manure. They should not be transferred to the field until two weeks after danger of frost is passed; if the spring be cold and backward, it is better to keep the plants under the protecting cloth. Some vegetable-raisers may object to this method as being expensive, but let us see if it is. In the first place, it does away with the first two plowings. In the second place, the plants are further advanced, and so less subject to insect and fungus attacks. The striped cucumber beetle and the cucumber aphis rarely get a start on pot-grown plants. The amount of seed required will be reduced to a minimum. The most important consideration, however, is that the first pickings will be two weeks or a month earlier than they would have been had the seed been planted in the field. The greatest drawback is that it requires skill on the part of the "cuke-grower" that is not demanded by the old method.

SOIL AND PREPARATION OF THE FIELD.

A light sandy loam on a southern slope will be found admirable. The low flat lands of bottoms should be avoided. If a warm sandy loam is not accessible, an upland clay may be used as a second choice; this will raise as large a crop, or larger than a sandy loam, but will not be quite so early.

Plow the field to a medium depth, turning it over well. While this vegetable is partial to the finer grades of fertilizer, it will thrive on coarser material than many other plants. Any form of decaying organic material may be utilized to advantage. Lay the field off in rows six feet apart, and make the hills from four to six feet apart in the row. Two weeks before the field is to be planted, the rows and checks

CUCUMBERS.

are laid off, and wherever a hill is to be planted, the amount of fertilizer desired is dropped and worked in thoroughly. If commercial or other concentrated fertilizer is to be used, send the best hand available to scatter the fertilizer in a three-foot circle about the check; then tell him that his wages depend on the completeness with which he works in the fertilizer; when he gets through, choose another hand equally as good, and give him to understand that he has to go over the whole field and do the work better than the former laborer did. When he has gone over the field, put a third man on to it, and impress on him the necessity of excelling his predecessors. By this time, if the orders have been emphatic, the fertilizer may be worked in sufficiently. We never suffer from over fertilizing in the field, but frequently ruin a crop by improper fertilization.

Two weeks after fertilizing a field, it is usually safe to plant either the seed or the plants. If the seed is planted, about a dozen should be dropped in a hill. When the plants begin to run, the hill should be reduced to from two to four plants. Some of the missing hills may be supplied by lifting a part of a full hill on a hoe and setting it to place. If plants are set out, remove the pots and set the ball of earth that was in the pot an inch below the surface of the ground.

CULTIVATING.

Whether the seed is planted in the field or plants from a cold frame set out, the land must be in best of tilth. If warm, dry weather follows the time of planting, the first plowing may be delayed ten days, but by this time the cultivator should be used on each side of the row, and a week after this plowing the rows should be crossed. This plowing is not so much to kill out young weeds as to get air into the soil; and to give the sun a chance to warm it up. If rains occur soon after planting, no time should be lost in loosening the soil; this will help to let off the surplus water besides achieving the same objects stated before, viz.: aerate and warm the soil. These hard rains of winter and spring that occur in the Lower South are a greater drawback in vegetable growing than they seem to the majority of people in that business. If plants have been set out, the plowing should not be delayed so long.

It is usually not necessary to cultivate the middles oftener than twice a month, just often enough to keep the land in good condition. As the vines grow out from the hills, as centers, the "middles" will decrease in width until finally the hills meet and plowing must be suspended. In case a vine begins to "run" too much, cut off its tips; this will cause new laterals to be formed and the hill to grow compact. It is not good to move a vine, as this loosens its hold and gives the wind a chance to mutilate it. If the hill is kept compact by heading in all runners the vines will cling to one another, and obviate the danger from being blown about.

PICKING AND PACKING.

Cukes are "ripe" when the blossom end has filled out well. (See Fig. 24.) It is best to let them get as large as possible without letting the seed harden. As soon as the shell around the seed begins to harden they are no longer salable; this can be learned by testing a few. One will find that the appearance will differ with the variety. If by chance or otherwise some have been left on the vines too long, they should be pulled as soon as possible. A ripening cucumber saps the vitality out of a vine to a remarkable degree. Culls and wormy ones should also be removed immediately. Often culls can be sold in the local market to advantage, but it will not pay to ship them. Some cuke-growers find it profitable to give the best of them to the railroad employees and laborers.

Fig. 24.

The ordinary vegetable crate is used for shipping. They should be picked while dry, taken to the packing house, sorted and crated. They are laid in quickly and evenly; pressed down with a lever, and the crate nailed. The product should not be bruised and not be loose enough to shake in the crate in transit. It is necessary to pick a field three times a week. The amount that an acre will produce seems incredible to those who have not raised a full crop; while two to three hundred crates may be considered a fair crop, we have reports of six hundred, eight hundred, and even nine hundred crates to the acre.

SAVING SEED.

This seed may be kept ten years without serious loss of vitality, though fresh is preferred. If the shipping season should be short, the later part of the crop may be allowed to ripen. Saving seed is a simple, easy and profitable employment. The ripe cucumbers are gathered, of course only the perfectly formed ones being selected, and taken to the packing-house. Cut the fruit into halves lengthwise and scrape out the seed and pulp into a barrel, which may be filled half or three-fourths full, but not more, as the fermenting would cause it to run over. Let the material remain in the barrel five days to ferment the mucilage off the seed. It should be stirred once or twice a day to mix the whole thoroughly, so the fermentation will go on evenly. At the end of this time the seed can be washed clean.

If one has a hydrant or force-pump the work of cleaning seed can be greatly facilitated. A number 3 and a number 10 sieve should be provided beforehand for this work; these can be obtained from most of the hardware stores. Provide also a large tub in which the washing is to be done. Fill the tub with water; immerse the number three sieve into this; fill in some of the pulp from the barrel. While the sieve is under water the pulp is worked about to separate the seed; this being heavier passes through the seive, while most of the pulp and pieces of rind are caught. When nearly all the seed have passed through, rinse the sieve out and remove the pulp. Repeat the operation until a barrel of material has been worked through. Some of the pieces of pulp that passed through the sieve can be floated off by forcing water among the seed. Pour the seed into the number ten sieve and set aside to drain. Protecting cloth will be found excellent to dry the seed on; they may be spread out to the sun for a half day and complete the drying in shade. When the seed is thoroughly dry, winnow and finally sift out remaining heavy particles through the number ten sieve. Wrap and label securely. In our climate it will be advisable to look out for mice and roaches as well as moisture. Wrap the seed in glazed or in parchment paper and place in a tight box.

As stated before, this seed has great vitality, consequently we need not be uneasy if it has to be kept for two or three years. If the usual markets will not take it, we can open a market for ourselves in our own territory.

VARIETIES.

There are many varieties that are commendable for forcing, but for field culture none exceed in popularity the Improved White Spine. (See Fig. 24.) For home use an earlier variety, such as Early Russian or Early Cluster, may be raised.

FERTILIZER FORMULA.

Nitrogen .... 5 per cent.
Potash... ....8 "
Phosphoric acid... .... 7 "

Use 1000 to 1500 pounds of the above formula per acre.

Care must be exercised that it is thoroughly incorporated with the soil.

The following table will give the amounts of different fertilizers necessary to obtain the desired amount of each element:

Element.	Pounds of different material for one acre
Nitrogen.............	800 to 1200 lbs. cotton-seed meal; or 500 to 750 lbs. dried blood; or 400 to 600 lbs. nitrate of soda; or 250 to 325 lbs. sulphate of ammonia.
Potash...............	1000 to 1500 lbs. kainit; or 160 to 240 lbs. muriate of potash; or 160 to 240 lbs. sulphate of potash; or 300 to 450 lbs. sulphate of potash and sulphate of magnesia.
Phosphoric acid..	900 to 1300 lbs. acid phosphate; or 700 to 1000 lbs. dissolved bone.

The amounts of the above fertilizer elements should

be varied to suit the individual farm. If the land is rich in organic matter, the amount of nitrogenous elements should be decreased, as too much of it makes poor shippers and overgrown sizes, and tends to make the vines unfruitful.

If the shipping season is unusually prolonged, the bearing season may also be prolonged by sowing from 50 to 100 pounds per acre of nitrate of soda or sulphate of ammonia. This application should be made when the plants are perfectly dry, and preferable on a windy day. This precaution will reduce the number of leaves scalded to a minimum. If cotton seed meal has been used as a source of nitrogen, it will be found profitable to scatter two or three spoonfuls of nitrate of soda around the plants just after they appear above the ground or as they are set out. This will hasten them out of danger from insects.

MUSK MELONS.

SOIL AND PREPARATION.

The soil used for ordinary gardening will be found well adapted to this crop. While musk melons grow well on a stiff clay soil, they are later in maturing than on warm loam.

The ordinary preparation will give good results. The land should be plowed shallow, but all turned. If it is a light sandy loam, four furrows turned together will make a sufficient bed to plant on.

FIG. 25.

FIG. 26.

VARIETIES.

This vegetable has been so long in cultivation that the wild species is not known. Under the name musk melon, we have two forms—the short or turbinate-shaped (see Fig. 25), usually called nutmeg or musk melon; and the long form, usually called canteloupe (see Fig. 26). The latter are the stronger growers, and should have more room in the field.

For shipping, Jenny Lind, Emerald Gem, Nutmeg and Hackensack are good.

FERTILIZER FORMULA.

Nitrogen... .... 3 per cent.
Potash... .... 8 per cent.
Available phosphoric acid .... 8 per cent.

Use 1000 to 1500 pounds of the above formula per acre. If the soil is poor in nitrogenous matter, increase the nitrogen to four per cent.

The following table gives the amounts of different fertilizers that may be used to obtain as much of each element as the formula calls for:

Element.	Pounds of different material for one acre.
Nitrogen	500 to 750 lbs. cotton-seed meal; or 300 to 450 lbs. dried blood; or 225 to 350 lbs. nitrate of soda; or 200 to 300 lbs. sulphate of ammonia.
Potash	1000 to 1500 lbs. kainit; or 160 to 225 lbs. muriate of potash; or 160 to 225 lbs. sulphate of potash; or 300 to 450 lbs. sulphate of potash and sulphate of magnesia.
Phosphoric acid	800 to 1200 lbs. acid phosphate; or 700 to 1000 lbs. dissolved bone.

PLANTING AND CULTIVATING.

This crop may be treated like cucumbers and planted in pots, and then be set out in the field, or the seed may be planted in the field.

Make the rows six feet apart and put the hills from three to six feet apart in the row, according to the variety. If the land is rich, or a liberal amount of fertilizer has been used, the plants may be allowed to grow as close as a foot in the row. Drop from four to eight seeds where a plant is desired, and the time the vines begin to run they should be thinned out to the desired stand.

The cultivation must be shallow, but kept up constantly and the weeds kept down.

MARKETING.

It is necessary to pack this crop in crates. The smaller varieties may be shipped in vegetable crates and the larger ones in hundred pound crates.

Since the inauguration of rapid transit for vegetables, this crop can be shipped profitably during spring.

SAVING SEED.

No difficulty will arise from planting musk melons and watermelons in the same field. There is no danger of hybridizing these two species, but seed should not be saved where different varieties of musk melons have been planted in the same field.

Save the seed in the same way as directed for cucumbers.

The seed may be kept ten years without losing its vitality, under proper conditions.

GHERKINS.

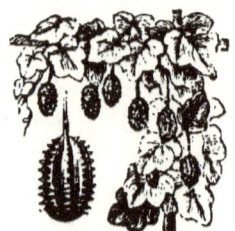

Fig. 27.

Thi, small cucumber-like fruit is becoming popular as a pickle. (See Fig. 27.) They are desirable only as pickles, and as such will take the place of small cucumbers very nicely. The plant is so much more hardy than the cucumber, that it can be grown in many localities where cucumbers fail. In the manner of seeding, planting out and care, follow the directions given for cucumbers. When the vines begin to run, they are usually furnished with some kind of trellis or other support. This is quite an advantage, as it brings the fruit in sight and raises it from the ground, making it more easily picked and kept from getting sandy or dirty.

SQUASHES.

It is believed by many persons that when melons and squashes, melons and canteloupes, melons and cucumbers, or any other combination of these are planted together, they will produce hybrids. Bees and other insects are supposed to carry the pollen which effect this combination. While this belief is firmly impressed on many gardeners, no botanist or horticulturist has yet been able to produce these hybrids. In no case has the fruit set, but the blossoms have fallen as though not fertilized. The above remarks should not be construed to mean that different varieties of squashes will not cross with one another, because this occurs freely.

SELECTING THE SOIL.

A good cucumber soil is also a good squash soil. Very rich land with but little sand in the soil is not adapted for squashes; there will be an abundance of fruit, but it will be insipid and will rot easily. A piece of well-drained sandy muck land raises heavy crops of good fruit. For shipping, the early varieties are about the only ones that pay.

Squashes have one advantage over melons and cucumbers, in that they can be grown on freshly-broken land. All that is necessary is to see to it that the land is kept in a well-worked condition. It does not pay to neglect this crop any more than with any other.

Almost any kind of decaying organic matter will make a good manure for this crop; it responds to good treatment, however. The plant should not be allowed to exhaust the fertilizer which is in the soil before more that is in an available form is applied. If it is well balanced, there will be no trouble arising from too much being used; but care must be exercised not to use too much nitrogen. Mr. J. J. H. Gregory, who is the best authority on squash-raising in this country, applies an amount of manure that seems very large indeed, but at the close of his discussion on fertilizers, he makes this pointed statement: "Catch a farmer of that class (one who fertilizes heavily) going backwards and putting less and less manure on his ground, what a phenomenon he would be. No; the progress of all enterprising farmers is in one direction. By extra manuring, the possibilities of receiving extra paying returns are far greater in agricultural than in commercial life, as figures will readily show, though the popular belief is directly the contrary."

Of all the plants that we have discussed, these can best stand top-dressing in fertilizing, and are best adapted to hill fertilization. A plan that has long been followed, is to dig a circle about two feet in diameter and about a foot deep, then fill in a lot of fertilizer with the earth taken out; this will make a mole-hill shaped mound when finished. The seeds are then planted on top. This involves a great deal of unnecessary work with no advantage. A better way is to make the hills where wanted, fertilize this heavily and mix well with the soil, but do not stir more than six or eight inches deep, as the roots are surface-feeders and should not be coaxed into the soil. The second application should be made when the vines begin to run, and must be placed some distance from the hill.

FERTILIZER FORMULA.

Nitrogen ....4 per cent.
Potash ....8 per cent.
Available phosphoric acid..........6 per cent.

Use 1000 to 1500 pounds of the above formula to the acre. If nitrate of soda is used to supply the nitrogen, several applications will have to be given.

It will be better, however, to use some less soluble form.

The following amounts of fertilizers will give the desired amount of each element:

Element.	Pounds of different material for one acre.
Nitrogen	650 to 1000 lbs. cotton-seed meal; or 400 to 600 lbs. dried blood; or 300 to 400 lbs. nitrate of soda; or 200 to 300 lbs. sulphate of ammonia.
Potash	1000 to 1500 lbs. kainit; or 160 to 225 lbs. muriate of potash; or 160 to 225 lbs. sulphate of potash; or 300 to 450 lbs. sulphate of potash, and sulphate of magnesia.
Phosphoric acid.	600 to 750 lbs. acid phosphate; or 500 to 600 lbs. dissolved bone

FIG. 28.

FIG. 29.

VARIETIES.

For the Northern market, the summer class should be planted. Early White Bush (see Fig. 28), Golden Custard (see Fig. 29), and Yellow Crookneck. The first and last named are the better sellers.

For home use and home markets, the fall sorts will be the more profitable. Early Orange Marrow, Winter Crookneck, Marblehead and Hubbard are desirable varieties.

PLANTING.

The hills are planted six by six or eight by eight feet apart and the seed dropped directly in the field; about two and a half pounds are required for an acre. There is much less danger from insects than in the case of cucumbers. It is well to drop about six seeds to the hill, and when the danger from insects is past, thin out to three plants.

When a crop is wanted early, it can be obtained by following the directions given under the discussion of Cucumbers. One should begin with a four-inch pot, however. Some gardeners cut sod, turn it upside down and plant seed on these in a cold frame or hotbed. This practice does very well with those who give careful attention to the growing of squashes, but with the novice it fails oftener than it succeeds. The one great point to be kept in mind is, that the plant should never become checked in its growth.

CULTIVATING.

Soon after the earlier leaves appear, the plant seems to become weak near the ground, and the whole plant is easily tossed about from one side to another by the wind, and often plants are broken off or at least severely bruised. This can be remedied by drawing the earth up to the plants with a hoe, but this should not be carried on so far as to make a hill for them to stand on; just enough should be drawn up to hold the plant in place.

As soon as the plants are set in the field, or as soon as the seedlings appear above the ground, the horse and plow should be set to work in the field. If it is in a state of good cultivation, there is not much use for a hoe; the filling referred to before can be done with a cultivator. If the season is dry, the top of the soil should be stirred often to conserve the moisture. During a drouth, the weeds should be jealously kept down, as they are just so many leaks to moisture in the soil.

When the vines begin to "run" they grow very rapidly—some have been ascertained to grow fourteen inches in twenty-four hours; so the field should be kept in the best condition before this time. It is a bad practice to pick the vines up and turn them from their course; they are subsequently so easily broken up by the wind that little or no fruit sets.

When the price of land is high, squashes are planted as a second crop, or at the edge of some other crop, as corn.

MARKETING.

This crop is usually marketed in barrels or boxes. While many acres have been grown in the South, it is not a crop to be relied upon for profit. The gardeners in the North are able to store and keep their fall crop over winter, so it will be late in the spring before there is great demand for the Southern-grown produce. It is a good crop, however, to raise for home market, and they are so easily grown that every farmer or gardener can have them for family use.

The seed does not remain good as long as that of cucumbers, but it has been known to be vital at six years old and again spoiled at three. The best way is to test it before planting.

For many uses in the kitchen, this crop can be evaporated or it can be canned; the business has now grown to large proportions.

PUMPKINS.

As this crop is not one that brings in money, it usually has to content itself by growing on such land as is either not wanted for other crops or as can be spared. Not that a rich warm loam will not produce the largest crop, but that it pays better when planted to many other crops. Consequently, pumpkins are usually planted on new land that has not been subdued or on waste land.

In cultivating, care should be taken not to tear the soil up deeply about the plants that have begun to run. Like other plants of the gourd family, it is a shallow feeder. Any one desiring to plant a crop will find that the directions given for squashes are approximately correct for this one.

There are two varieties with several sorts under each variety; the one variety is coarse-grained and large, used to feed stock; the other variety is often called the Yankee pumpkin—it is fine-grained, hard, and sweet; it is also called the pie-pumpkin. The later variety is the one planted for marketing in New England.

Only a very few can be marketed in the South.

WATERMELONS.

SOIL.

This plant will flourish and make an excellent crop on warm sandy soil. Heavy or soggy land should not be chosen, nor will thirsty soil produce a good crop, but this plant has a wider range of soil than any other that we raise for market. The profits from raising watermelons are so small usually that from inferior soil they approach the vanishing point. Then, again, the early shipments, as a rule, bring good returns, while the later ones are liable to be a loss.

The plowing should be shallow but thorough; while the roots do not penetrate deeply, they grow out for a long distance from the hill, and in no case should the fertilizer be so placed as to coax the roots to an unnatural stratum.

FERTILIZER FORMULA.

Nitrogen .... 3 per cent.
Potash .... 8 per cent.
Available phosphoric acid .... 8 per cent.

Use from 800 to 1200 pounds of the above formula per acre. If the soil is rich in nitrogenous matter, omit this element altogether. Too much nitrogen makes overgrown melons, poor shippers, and a product with an insipid taste. From the foregoing, it should not be considered that fertilizer can produce a fine crop from a poor variety, but by properly balancing the fertilizer we can often raise a fine crop where otherwise we would fail.

The following table gives the amounts of different fertilizers that may be used to obtain as much of each element as the formula calls for :

Element.	Pounds of different material for one acre.
Nitrogen............	400 to 600 lbs. cotton seed meal; or 250 to 350 lbs. dried blood; or 175 to 250 lbs. nitrate of soda; or 150 to 200 lbs. sulphate of ammonia.
Potash............	800 to 1200 lbs. kainit; or 125 to 200 lbs. muriate of potash; or 125 to 200 lbs. sulphate of potash; or 250 to 300 lbs. sulphate of potash and sulphate of ammonia.
Phosphoric acid.	650 to 900 lbs. acid phosphate; or 500 to 800 lbs. dissolved bone.

VARIETIES.

In choosing a variety to raise, be sure that the meat is solid and the rind hard and strong, if wanted for distant market. The following varieties will be found good: Dixie, Kolb Gem, Florida Favorite, Pride of Georgia, and Rattlesnake.

For home use and local markets, much will depend on the local demand; usually, these want a small, or medium-sized melon, very sweet; thin-rind and red-fleshed. The following varieties will be found to have red flesh: Black Spanish, Dark Icing, Ice Cream, and Mountain Sweet. If the last mentioned is desired, be sure that seed from a good strain is obtained.

PLANTING.

Lay the land off in checks about six by six feet and use the fertilizer in the hill. Let no one deceive himself into the belief that it is enough to run a plow through the hill once or twice to mix the fertilizer with the soil. The melon-grower who uses commercial fertilizer must, sooner or later, learn that to mix the fertilizer thoroughly with the soil means about three times as much work as the majority of growers usually put on to it. The fertilizer should be scattered in a circle about three feet in diameter about the place where the hill is to stand. Use the fertilizer a week or ten days before planting.

A crop may be brought in early by using flowerpots and potting soil as described for cucumbers, but the pots should be a size larger than for cucumbers.

When seed is planted in the field, it may be planted in a shorter time after fertilizing than when plants are set out. Drop eight or twelve seeds in a hill; insects and vermin will destroy so many that but few will have to be thinned out. If cotton-seed meal has been used as a source of nitrogen (and this is advisable), a teaspoonful of nitrate of soda may be scattered in the hill just after the seedlings have appeared above the ground, or as the plants are set out. This will stimulate the plants to a rapid growth, and get them out of the way of insects.

CULTIVATING.

All cultivation should be shallow, merely to keep the surface mellow and free from weeds. As soon as practicable after heavy rains, the field should be plowed, and, when no rains occur, the field should be plowed every week or ten days, depending upon the kind of land. It is not necessary to plow all the middles while the plants are small, but weeds should not be allowed to go to seed; but if the weather is dry, the middles must be worked to conserve the moisture in the soil, and all weeds kept down, as each one of these is a leak to so much soil moisture. As the plants grow larger, the cultivation has to be pushed farther to the middles until finally the plants meet across the rows, when plowing must be discontinued. If tall weeds grow in the field after this, they should be cut off, not pulled, as the vines are fastened to these by their tendrils and the vines must not be disturbed.

MARKETING.

This is a simple operation, and yet many fail from

various causes. Experience alone can guide one as to how ripe the crop must be to reach the market in time from his locality.

In loading a car, size the melons and place the smallest on the bottom ; these can stand the weight better, and if one is smashed the loss is less than if a large one were destroyed.

SAVING SEED.

Only the finest specimens, and on vines free from disease, should be selected. Melons intended for seed may be marked by a scratch in the rind ; and as soon as the fruit is full grown, all the other melons on that vine should be removed, so as to throw as much vitality into the seed as possible.

Let the melon become dead ripe, and remove to the packing house. Cut it in two and remove the flesh and seed. Drop the flesh into a tub and mash it well without injuring the seed. Turn this into a barrel and stand in a warm place ; in twenty-four hours, stir the contents to make them as even as possible. In about forty-eight hours the material will have fermented enough to macerate the flesh; the seed may then be removed by washing in a No. 2 sieve.

The seed must not be allowed to remain in the barrel longer than about sixty hours, as the heat generated is liable to make them sprout.

As soon as the seed is washed, it should be drained and dried quickly without any heat.

This seed has been kept for twelve years without losing its vitality.

GOURD.

Under this name we have several species, usually distinguished by some adjective, as bottle gourd, dish-cloth gourd, nest egg gourd, etc. All of these grow spontaneously in rich lots or fields, after they have been introduced. While dippers and other implements made from them are rather crude, they need not be despised, as many a ten cent may be saved to the gardener using them.

Plant the seed late in spring where the vine is wanted. Choose some place as a fence or lattice for it to run on. An out-of-the-way place in a wood yard or a back porch are usually employed. The nest-egg gourd has a smaller fruit and a smaller vine than the bottle or dipper gourd.

ENGLISH PEA.

This vegetable is very generally cultivated in the South for winter and early spring market. It is a staple crop, and as it requires very little attention it is a favorite with many vegetable-growers. The land should be well prepared, though not deeply, about the last of October or in November; the fertilizer scattered along the row and mixed with the soil. This crop will stand a light frost and grow even in quite cold weather. A temperature of 24°F. will injure open flowers and pods, but will not hurt the vines unless in an active growing state.

For shipping purposes the dwarf varieties should be chosen. The American Wonder and Blue Beauty do exceedingly well. The large number of varieties offered for sale often leads to confusion, but the two named above may be regarded as trustworthy.

For home use it is often desirable to sow the tall-growing varieties; these are later but usually more prolific. The land is prepared in the same way as for the dwarf varieties. It is much better to make two long rows of these than four half rows. If it becomes necessary to plant these in a body—that is, plant more than two rows alongside of one another—the alternate rows should be planted farther apart, so as to have them by twos. When they have reached a height of ten to fourteen inches it will be time to stake them. Let the two near rows be staked so they will mat together leaving an abundance of space to pass between the alternate rows. As nearly all the peas will form on the outside or to the light, the picking will be quite easy.

A light warm soil is very desirable for winter crops. If one uses a seed drill a row should be made up of three or four drills about one inch apart. This will give them a chance to hold to one another and thus form supports. The ordinary practice is to make a row about six inches wide, by scattering the seed along a furrow, and covering about an inch deep. Peas sown later than the first of January are liable to come into competition with those grown farther north.

Cultivation is needed more to get air into the soil than to keep the weeds down. During cultivtaion the soil should be gradually worked up to the row so as to leave them hilled up at the last plowing. The distance between the rows should be about twenty inches for strong soil.

FERTILIZER FORMULA.

Available phosphoric acid ..... 7 per cent.
Potash .... 7 per cent.
Nitrogen ... .3 per cent.

Use 600 to 1000 pounds to the acre.

For this crop it will be found desirable to use mineral fertilizer rather than compost. If nitrate of soda is used it will require two applications—one at the time of sowing, and the second just as the first flower buds begin to show. Cotton-seed meal can be used as a source of nitrogen before planting, as a portion of a compost fertilizer. Nitrate of soda will cause the vines to make a vigorous growth, so should not be applied when a frost is looked for.

The following amounts of fertilizing materials may be used to obtain the amounts of each of the fertilizer elements called for in the formula:

Element.	Pounds of different materials for one acre.
Nitrogen	300 to 500 lbs. cotton-seed meal; or 180 to 300 lbs. dried blood; or 120 to 200 lbs. nitrate of soda; or 100 to 150 lbs. sulphate of ammonia.
Potash	500 to 900 lbs. of kainit; or 80 to 140 lbs. muriate of potash; or 90 to 150 lbs. sulphate of potash; or 160 to 240 lbs. sulphate of potash, and sulphate of magnesia.
Phosphoric acid	420 to 700 lbs. acid phosphate; or 350 to 600 lbs. dissolved bone.

BEAN.

Fig. 30.

The bean is a tender annual, and does not grow to perfection in cold weather. Its value as a food has long been recognized, but the people in this country are slow in adopting it as food for animals, though for household consumption it is used extensively. In Europe and Asia, it is used largely as feed. The main reason for its not being used more extensively in the United States is that much time is consumed in gathering. As soon as we shall be able to harvest it by horse-power, we will use it largely in feeding domestic animals.

Seedsmen divide beans into two classes—the bush beans and the pole beans. Each of these classes requires quite different treatment. We will consider the bush or dwarf kind first.

BUSH BEAN.

This is the kind (see Fig. 30) that is used for shipping purposes, as snap-beans or snaps. In some portions of the South, the growing of string-beans is a lucrative class of gardening. All beans are tender and sensitive to cold, even when it is not severe enough to freeze. Only those portions of the South that are free from frosts and long cold spells can grow them for midwinter market; in other portions, late fall and early spring crops pay well.

VARIETIES.

One of the earliest and most hardy is the Mohawk. A little later, but probably more prolific variety, is the Valentine. A variety fine for table use, and one good for marketing, is the Golden Wax (see Fig. 30). It has one drawback, which will be overcome in time, and that is that the seed is expensive.

The green podded varieties are more popular among gardeners because of a general belief that they are hardier than the yellow podded ones. There is less danger of getting poor varieties in beans than in many other vegetables.

SOIL.

For early winter crop a light sandy soil is most valuable, while for a fall crop a heavier soil may be used to advantage. The land should be prepared moderately deep, and need not be in a high state of tilth. Any decaying vegetable matter that happens to be on the field may be left there.

FERTILIZER FORMULA.

Available phosphoric acid .... 7 per cent.
Potash ....7 per cent.
Nitrogen .... 3 per cent.

On poor land use 1000 to 1500 pounds of the above formula per acre. If the land is rich in vegetable matter, the nitrogen may be omitted. While beans are able to assimilate atmospheric nitrogen, they are not able to grow well in a soil free of this element.

To obtain the amounts of different fertilizer elements called for in the above formula, the following materials may be used :

Element.	Pounds of different materials for one acre.
Nitrogen............	300 to 400 lbs. dried blood; or 200 to 300 lbs. nitrate of soda; or 500 to 750 lbs. cotton-seed meal; or 150 to 200 lbs. sulphate ammonia.
Potash............	900 to 1200 lbs. kainit; or 150 to 200 lbs. muriate of potash; or 150 to 200 lbs. sulphate of potash; or 300 to 450 lbs. sulphate of potash and sulphate of magnesia.
Phosphoric acid..	700 to 1000 lbs. acid phosphate; or 600 to 900 lbs. dissolved bone.

PLANTING AND CULTIVATING.

When the crop is intended for snaps, make the rows two and a half feet apart, and thin the plants to four or six inches apart in the row. Make the row as straight as possible; this will save labor in cultivating.

In sections where artesian wells may be employed to irrigate, the rows should be run on contours. When such contours lines have been established, they will serve as guides by which the irrigating system is laid out. A very simple and effective method has been employed with good success by some vegetable growers in South Florida. The field, after the contour lines have been located, is thrown up in beds wide enough to hold but two rows. These beds are made by using a large two horse plow and throwing up a head-land for every two rows of the crop to be planted. This leaves a double open furrow for every two rows. When the water is turned into such an open furrow, it moistens the land quite thoroughly. Such work requires a great amount of water, and is not practicable where the supply is limited. Under such a plan, the two rows on a bed are made only eighteen or twenty inches apart, while the distance between them on separate beds is correspondingly greater.

All cultivating in a bean-field should be shallow unless they are planted in a heavy soil, but it should be frequent, especially in rainy weather (this, of course, does not refer to clay soil). As soon as the bloom appears abundantly, it is time to stop cultivating, at least near the plants.

PREPARING FOR MARKET.

Snaps are picked any time during the day when the dew is off and they are not wet from rains. As soon as the beans in the pod are about half grown, or before the pods begin to be hard, is the time they should be picked.

They are taken to the packing-house and allowed to stand free to the air for an hour or so to loose their brittleness. The packing is simple. The pile is worked over more or less closely and all culls removed, at the same time they are straitened more or less and placed in an ordinary vegetable crate. The crates are pressed down just enough to keep the product from shaking about.

HARVESTING.

If the crop is to ripen, it will be found more convenient to plant them in hills, but these should be proportionately farther apart in the row. As soon as nearly all the pods are ripe, the plants may be cut off with a scythe or a grass-mower. The gathering is usually best accomplished by collecting the vines on forks and placing them in small piles at convenient distances. When thoroughly dry, they are stacked, and later threshed either by machine or by hand. The hand-threshed bean usually contains fewer broken ones, and hence sell for a higher price. Often the pods are picked as they ripen, but this process is too expensive for any but seed beans.

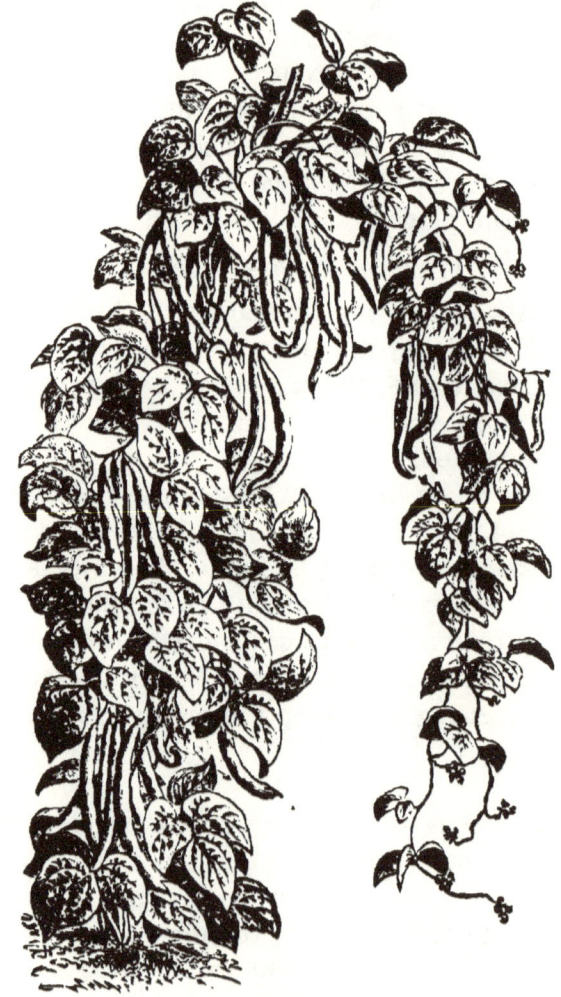

FIG. 31.

POLE BEANS.

The pole beans (see Fig. 31) require a much richer soil than the bush beans, and are rarely used for shipping purposes. These beans are more desirable for family use, but are somewhat later in maturing, so both kinds should be planted for home use. The pole limas are more desirable, but there is much difficulty in the pods setting.

The early preparation of the soil is the same as for the low-growing forms. Lay the land off four by four or six by six feet, fertilize the checks thoroughly, and after the fertilizer is well incorporated, plant the seed. Plant from one to four beans to the hill; vary the number of plants to suit the strength of the land. Such ordinary care as is given the garden crops will be sufficient. As soon as the vines begin to run, they should be staked. In this matter, it is best to set the stakes so the tops of four will come together, and tie them; in this way, they will support one another. By staking them in squares, the space between the rows arched together must be cultivated by hand, but the vines will soon shade the ground, thus preventing further growth of weeds.

VARIETIES.

Under this head, we will include the bush limas, though they belong properly among the bush or snap beans. There are several varieties of these offered for sale, and all are of an excellent quality.

Among the pole beans we can recommend the Early Jersey, Siebert's Early, and Horticultural. Among ordinary pole beans we have Dutch Case Knife, Scarlet Runner, and Old Homestead.

While the bush lima and pole beans come in too late for distant markets, they are among the most desirable and substantial food for the kitchen garden. For local markets, they are unexcelled, and comparatively new in our section.

PEANUT.

This plant has been introduced but recently to cultivation. It is safe to predict that in fifty years from now it will be one of the staple products of the South. It is already such in Virginia and the Carolinas. By chemists it is regarded as being of the highest value as an article of food for man and the lower animals. It is said to be more nearly a complete food than any other crop that we raise. The oil has been used in many places instead of olive oil, and those who are enthusiasts on the subject say that it is just as sweet and good. The pure oil is nearly colorless, with a slight odor that is not unpleasant, and a taste resembling that of olive oil. It is largely used in soap making, and can be used for lubricating purposes, also for burning. One bushel of unhulled peanuts yield about a gallon of oil. The residue, after expressing the oil, makes a good oil cake for stock, also a good fertilizer, but it is too valuable for that purpose. Beside the roasted peanut we have the peanut coffee, peanut bread, and peanut hay. Pigs fatten rapidly when turned into a pindar or peanut field. The hay will be referred to again under the head of harvesting.

SOIL AND PREPARATION.

Peanuts want light, sandy soil, quite well drained, but not dry. A warm location is preferred. It is affirmed by persons who ought to know that there must be a quantity of lime in the soil for this plant to do well, but there is no record of experiments at hand that proves this conclusively. In the absence of any evidence to the contrary, we shall have to accept the teaching as presented. The marls from the seacoast are highly recommended.

The preparation of the field is very similar to that of the usual field crop, with the exception that it should be more thorough. Deep plowing is essential where drought may occur during growing season.

PLANTING.

Before planting, the pods are broken open between the thumb and fingers; care being taken not to injure the kernels. After seed has been prepared it must be stored in small packages to keep it from heating, but care must also be taken to keep it from becoming too dry. When many acres are planted by one person it becomes quite a task and also a risk to keep the seed after it is prepared. While the seed is being hulled it is at the same time selected; all the poorly formed and bad kernels being thrown out. Two bushels in the pod will give seed enough to plant an acre.

In Virginia and the Carolinas, it is necessary to be very careful about the time of planting; if a cold spell follows the planting, the seed is liable to fail; if the planter waits until cold weather is past, the heaviest portion of the crop is liable to be frozen in the fall. The matter of replanting in those States is a doubtful investment. In Lower South there is no disadvantage in waiting until the weather and soil are warm enough to ensure speedy germination. The seed should be tested, however, before it is committed to the ground; it will relieve much uneasiness. This can be done easily in a cold frame or a large shallow box, which can be protected from the cold.

The rows are made about three feet apart and the seed planted one to two feet apart on the row. The land being in a good state of cultivation, it is not difficult to lay off the rows and then make dots in which to drop the seed. On clay soil the row must be raised slightly above the general level, so the seed will be about on the level of the land. The seed should be planted about an inch deep; if the soil is sandy or light it will be better to plant deeper.

A handy implement called a dotter is used by peanut planters to mark the place where seed is to be dropped. It is made by fixing pegs or blocks to the rim of a wheel. The blocks or pegs are put as far apart as the hills are to be. Often the wheels are made by sawing off the end of a large tree; with two of these two rows may be dotted at once. The blocks or pegs make a small pit in the ground, into which the seed is dropped one at a time. Some planters drop two seeds in a dot, but this is not usually necessary, if the seed is quite certain to grow. As a laborer drops the seed he covers it with his foot.

In about two weeks after planting, the field should be examined and any missing hills replanted.

The time of planting depends on the weather, but it is some time between the middle of April and the middle of May.

CULTIVATION.

The field is put into thorough tilth before planting, and is kept in this way so as not to give the weeds a chance to get the crop down. A week or ten days after the field has been planted, it should be plowed or cultivated; some use a small turning plow to throw a light furrow onto the row and then drag it down again, thus killing the weeds and keeping the soil mellow and without damaging many peanut plants. It does not matter so much what kind of an instrument we use so long as we keep the soil mellow and deep and do not allow weeds to grow. In many sections it is better to plant the field in checks. One thing should be kept in mind constantly; that weeds are very difficult to be cleared out after the vines have begun to bush.

In general, the level or flat culture will be found better in light sandy soil. Under this form of cultivation the soil does not dry out as much as in hill culture. A second plowing and weeding is given within ten days or two weeks after the first; this is gauged more by the necessity of the case than by the time elapsing. The ground must be mellow and free from weeds. After the second plowing, the hoe and the fingers have to be used considerably; the hills have begun to spread so that it is difficult to plow up to the plants. Care must be taken not to disturb them as they are preparing to produce flower buds, and any interference is liable to be detrimental to the yield. All grass and weeds coming up in the hill have to be pulled out by hand. The third and fourth plowings have to be carried on with still greater care than the second; the weedings at these times need more care also, on account of the crop-setting at that time. After this, shallow cultivation may be kept up until the vines meet across the row. If the land is quite level, the cultivation should be carried on so that when the season is over the rows will stand on slight mounds, then the trough between them will carry off the water during a rainy season and keep the crop dry. After a field is well established there is little danger from drought.

HARVESTING.

About two months after the last plowing the earlier nuts begin to ripen; if the season is dry the vines may be left in the field until the greater portion of the crop is ripe, as there is little danger from frost in our section; but in Virginia the crop has to be harvested before the frost falls, as the nuts and vines are both severely damaged by it. During a rainy fall it is necessary to watch the crop and harvest it before the earlier ripened nuts begin to sprout.

For removing the vines a plow with a long sweep is used. This shear or blade passes along on each side of the row under the nuts and cuts off all roots that pass into the ground. This implement may be likened to a stirring plow with the mould board removed. The depth that this shear works in the earth is regulated so as to be as shallow as possible and yet not cut any of the nuts.

Laborers follow the plow and raise the vines with a pitch fork, at the same time shaking off all the dirt from the roots and nuts. Two rows of vines are tossed together into a winrow. These are allowed to dry for a few hours and then stacked. A pole about seven feet long is put into the ground firmly and the vines piled around this. Before stacking, some sticks of wood are laid about the pole to keep the vines off the ground. The stacks are made as narrow as possible to give them a good chance to dry out. In about two or three weeks from the time of stacking, the crop will be ready to be picked. This is usually done by women or children, and is paid for by the bushel. The picking is an expensive operation, and it may be delayed, but if the hay is wanted it is best not to leave this out any longer than necessary. It is also well to have the nuts where they cannot be destroyed by insects and other animals. Where one has the barn-room it will be found cheaper to dry the crop well and then house it at once.

The smaller kinds fill the shell more completely, and so can be picked by machine, but there has been some objection raised by the retail dealers to buying the nuts that have been picked by machine, but this will disappear when the separator is perfected and when the nuts become so cheap that they cannot be picked by hand. Passing the hay through a separator, is said to improve it.

After the nuts have been picked they should be cleaned. This is done at factories. This process throws out all pops and saps, and also removes the dirt and sand. It would undoubtedly pay to have one of these recleaners in every neighborhood, and to be able to put the product on the market in the best shape possible. As soon as the crop is recleaned, it should be sacked in bags holding about a hundred pounds, or four bushels. They can be stored in this way and put on the market at any time.

The yield is from thirty to fifty bushels per acre. Many crops are reported as being greater than this; some reported as high as a hundred bushels per acre. The eleventh census gives the average yield for the United States as seventeen and six-tenth bushels. Besides the nuts, from one to two tons of excellent hay is usually obtained.

After the crop has been removed, hogs should be pastured on the field to feed on the nuts that were not gathered.

VARIETIES.

There is considerable variation in the varieties that are grown in various States of the Union, but the information regarding them is not easily obtained, nor can one obtain the different varieties readily. The plant is susceptible of great and easy variation, consequently a fine subject for plant-breeding.

The popular Virginia varieties are large podded, while the Tennessee varieties bear smaller pods and are earlier. A variety known as the African peanut has a small pod, while the kernel more nearly fills the pod. The Spanish peanut is more like the American variety, and is a favorite in Georgia, Florida and Louisiana.

There is a good field for investigation and improvement for some Southern enterprise in breeding up and systematizing the peanut.

FERTILIZER FORMULA.

Available phosphoric acid .... 5 per cent.
Potash .... 10 per cent.
Nitrogen .... 3 per cent.

Use 600 to 1,000 pounds of the above formula per acre.

Most of our land will not require nitrogenous fertilizer for this crop, and lime is usually recommended. Where the acid phosphate is used, there will probably be enough lime in this to satisfy the crop.

The following table will give the amounts of differerent fertilizer materials that may be used to supply the desired amounts of each element :

Element.	Pounds of different material for one acre.
Nitrogen............	300 to 500 lbs. cotton-seed meal; or 180 to 300 lbs. dried blood; or 120 to 200 lbs. nitrate of soda; or 100 to 150 lbs. sulphate of ammonia.
Potash..............	800 to 1,200 lbs. kainit; or 120 to 200 lbs. muriate of potash; or 125 to 210 lbs. sulphate of potash; or 250 to 400 lbs. sulphate of potash and sulphate of magnesia.
Phosphoric acid..	300 to 500 lbs. acid phosphate; or 250 to 400 lbs. dissolved bone.

THE GOOBER.

Botanically, the peanut is *Arachis hypogœa*, Willd., while the goober is *Voandzeia subtereanea*. The goober looks like a very large, one-seeded peanut. There are some sections of our country where this name is applied to the peanut.

The cultivation and general manipulation is the same as for the peanut. The crop has not been grown sufficiently to make very decided reports on it.

Either the peanut or the goober makes a good soiling plant, and one that is well worth careful attention from this standpoint and from that of an economic crop.

IRISH POTATOES.

This plant was introduced to Europe as a flower, and to be grown as such in gardens. The early pharmaceutists reported it as poisonous. But now it is the support of millions of human beings.

Where the summers are long, the sweet potatoes will meet with the more favor, but the Irish potato commands the greater price.

To raise Irish potatoes profitably in the South, it will be well to watch the crop in the potato growing sections of the North ; if the yield of the late crop has been good, the demand for new potatoes will be small and the market easily stocked, but if the yield of the late crop has been poor, there will be a steady demand for all the potatoes we can raise.

SOIL AND PREPARATION.

This crop can stand heavier land than the usual vegetable, but the soil must be fertile and deep. A bay head or muck land that has been drained and freed of sourness, will be found exceedingly well adapted to this crop. A cold, stiff, clayey soil usually fails to give a profitable return. If the land is not naturally moist, water will have to be supplied ; it is useless to try to raise a crop on dry land, but it will stand a very long drought if the substratum is not dry. Heavy soggy land will not produce a good crop until it is freed of water. On this point we can do no better than to quote Dr. Lawes, of the Rothamsted Experiment Station, England : "If you want to grow large crops of potatoes, you must be liberal in your supply of water as well as of food. The following will give you some idea of the importance of rainfall, even when the potatoes have an abundance of food. We grow potatoes continually upon the same land, using the same measures—namely: Three hundred pounds of sulphate of potash, soda, magnesia, superphosphate, with, in one case, 400 pounds of phosphate of ammonia, and in another, 550 pounds of nitrate of soda. The potash and phosphate are in excess of the requirements of the largest crop grown, so they are an accumulation in the soil. The nitrogen is also largely in excess of what the crop takes up, but this does not accumulate. Rainfall in inches:

May to October, five mo. 1881, 13½ in., yield 482 bush. per acre.
"   "   1882, 12½ " yield 397   "   "
"   "   1883, 13 " yield 401   "   "
"   "   1884, 9, " yield 222   "   "

In 1881, the rainfall was better distributed over the season than in 1883. Of course, I do not advocate the use of irrigation unless for the purpose of experiment, but merely wish to point out how important an abundant supply of rain is. The rainfall last year was fairly abundant for all other crops, but not for potatoes."

In preparing the land, all debris and rubbish should be removed. The plowing should be deep and thorough, so there will be no difficulty for the plants to find moisture. Thorough plowing will in a way compensate for a lack of nitrogenous fertilizer. This point is not usually accepted, but it seems to be established.

If the field is to be irrigated (and this should be done where it is possible), it may be thrown up in beds wide enough to hold two rows. The trenches between the rows are to guide the water. During a very wet season, this trench of about nine inches in depth is excellent for drainage, as it keeps the water from standing on the land. By this method the plants are fed from the bottom, and keep sending their roots downward to the stratum of even moisture.

SEED.

The common practice before definite work had been done in this line, was to plant the refuse or smaller tuber. This practice was probably the result of necessity arising from having used up all the choice product for food. Later, the practice was carried to the other extreme, and the largest tubers only were used; this is more commendable than the other practice, but it is not the rational stand. The greatest attention should be directed to the nature of the whole plant; it is more desirable to raise six or eight medium-sized tubers to the plant than to have one or two very large ones and the rest small and unmarketable. Another point to be borne in mind is, that the tubers shall ripen at one time, even at the expense of average size and total productiveness.

A great many tests have been made to ascertain whether the "seed" end or the "stem" end is more productive; up to the present, there has been no law discovered that will hold good for all places and for all planters. It is quite well established, however, that a large piece of the tuber will make stronger plants than a small one. Some experiments go to show that the yield is directly proportional to the size of the tuber used. This is probably a strong statement of the case, but there is certainly much nourishment in a large piece, and it will be able to carry the plant over several freezes, when that from a small piece would succumb. Some of the largest yields from a single tuber of a given weight have been obtained by growing sets, as in the case of sweet potatoes.

It is usually best to cut the tubers before planting. There are machines that cut, drop the pieces, and fertilize the ground all at once; such machines are used with a profit in the potato regions of the Northwest.

On well-cleared land, and where large areas are to be planted, it will pay to use them.

PLANTING.

If the planting is to be done by hand, care should be taken not to cut the tubers and leave them lying in a pile; even so small a heap as a bushel is liable to heat and to destroy the germinating powers of some pieces in twenty-four hours. If the tubers are cut several days beforehand, scatter them to dry; the moisture lost by evaporation is soon regained when planted, and without any perceptible loss in vigor of growth. Cut the tubers so as to give the eyes as much "meat" as possible; if the conditions are proper, only one or two eyes in each piece will start, the rest remain dormant.

If the field can be irrigated, it is laid off in beds about six feet wide; two rows about two feet apart are planted on these beds. Drop the potatoes about a foot in the row, cover with a plow, and if the land is loose, roll. Some people advise the use of lime or land plaster on the cut tubers when they are not used immediately, but this process is too slow where we have so much fine weather. When an irrigating plan is used, it is impossible to cultivate across the rows, so they should be made as straight as possible, so the plow can run very near the row. It is possible to raise a good crop of potatoes without hoeing them at all.

For fields that can not be irrigated, the rows may be made two and a half or three feet apart. Two by two feet is too close for good cultivation. Where labor is hard to obtain, it will be found cheaper to raise the crop in checks; in such a case, the rows may be marked out two and a half feet apart and the cross-marks two feet apart. If labor is cheap, the rows may be marked out three feet apart and the potatoes dropped about a foot apart in the row. Such fields usually have to be hoed once or twice. Cover the pieces with four or five inches of soil.

FERTILIZER.

While potatoes enjoy decaying vegetable matter, such as sod or turf, barn yard manure is rarely used on account of its tendency to produce scab. It is very difficult to make the soil too rich, but whether it will pay to use large quantities of commercial fertilizer, depends on the conditions of the markets and the grower.

FERTILIZER FORMULA.

Nitrogen...............................4 per cent.
Potash................................. 9 per cent.
Available phosphoric acid ..... 6 per cent.

Use from 800 to 1200 pounds of the above formula. When potatoes sell for a high price and the land is near market, it will be found profitable to use as much as 2000 pounds.

Stable manure should not be used, as it is liable to produce scab. It is usually affirmed that any fertilizer containing chlorin is detrimental to the quality of the tubers, but the reports on this point are conflicting. But while we are awaiting a settlement of this point, we will be safe if we use a high grade of sulphate of potash.

The following quantities of fertilizers will give the desired amounts of the elements:

IRISH POTATOES.

Element.	Pounds of different material for one acre.
Nitrogen	500 to 800 lbs. cotton-seed meal; or 350 to 500 lbs. dried blood; or 200 to 300 lbs. nitrate of soda; or 150 to 250 lbs sulphate of ammonia.
Potash	200 to 300 lbs. nitrate of potash;* or 150 to 225 lbs. sulphate of potash.
Phosphoric acid	500 to 700 lbs. acid phosphate; or 400 to 600 lbs. dissolved bone.

A number of experiments have been made by Mr. E. S. Carman to ascertain whether the fertilizer should be placed over or under the seed; the question was not wholly decided, but it seemed to be somewhat more favorable to the plan of putting it under. The roots of the potatoes do not penetrate the soil as deeply as those of some other crops, so the fertilizer should be in the row or in the hill. In whatever way the fertilizer be applied, no effort should be spared to have it well mixed with the soil.

CULTIVATION.

The cultivation is much the same as that for tomatoes, and should be carried on in the same way. When the potatoes are about to come through the ground a good harrowing with a smoothing harrow will destroy many weeds and will take the place of the first hoeing, or possibly do away with it altogether.

The cultivation should be deep and thorough. If the field is not irrigated, it will be safer to employ level culture. Hill culture is good in a rainy year, but it is quite disastrous in a very dry one. In case of a rainy season trenches can be made in various portions of the field to relieve it from the surplus water. By the time the tubers begin to form the field should be "laid away."

---

* When nitrate of potash is used, only one-third the amount of materials used for nitrogen need be employed. By referring to the table of Approximate Amounts of Different Fertilizers, it will be seen that the nitrate of potash contains 13 to 14 per cent. of nitrogen.

HARVESTING.

The time to harvest depends on the condition of the market. Usually the earliest crop brings the best returns; very early potatoes never fail to sell well. The marketing is done in ordinary crates. This is a staple crop, so it is not necessary to pay much attention to fine stencils and nice crates. The crates that are too dark for most vegetables may be employed, the buyers pay more attention to the product offered for sale than the style in which it comes.

It is not profitable to raise large quantities for the local market, unless one is engaged in the general vegetable business. The hotels throughout the South consume a considerable quantity, and their trade is worth soliciting. The time of harvesting is determined by the condition of the tuber; if the skin peels off easily, they will not carry to a distant market, and be in presentable condition.

During the time that the crop brings a fancy price it will pay to dig them by hand with a fork, but when the profits are small and the crops large it will be found more profitable to use horse power. A favorite way is to plow them out with a common two horse turning plow, and then have the hands gather those in sight and to work the hills over as they are found. A more successful method is to use a potato digger. A cheap form is simply a large bull-tongue plow with iron rods projecting back to separate the potatoes and the soil. The machine is simple, but saves much labor and does efficient work. There are also much more elaborate machines, that dig and elevate the potatoes to a wagon at once, thus reducing the labor to a minimum, but these are not operated easily unless the land has been well cleared.

STORING.

In colder climates all that is necessary is to keep the potatoes from freezing, and usually they will remain sound until spring. As soon as warm weather approaches they begin to sprout. This may be prevented by keeping the cellar cool. In the South the matter of keeping them stored is not quite so simple, as the temperature is usually so high that germination begins soon after ripening. A very successful way of keeping potatoes for family use is to kill the buds, and then barrel the tubers to prevent excessive evaporation. One-half to one per cent. sulphur acid will accomplish the above. The potatoes are placed in the liquid used for an hour and then removed to dry. Of course, this will remove all vitality of the buds, and they can be used for food only. The operation kills many germs of decay at the same time, and in this much it acts as a preservative. Another excellent way is to keep the tubers in thoroughly dried sand, to which one part in four of air-slacked lime has been added. This me hod has an advantage in that their germinating power is not destroyed.

GENERAL REMARKS.

A great many different methods of cultivation and general treatment with a view of lessening the amount of labor or increasing the yield, have been tried, but most of these have fallen short of a general success. The methods of planting and cultivating are practically the same throughout the United States.

The large yields that one reads about are produced by persons who have served their apprenticeship at this kind of gardening. One should not expect to raise a heavy crop until he is well acquainted with the fields to be used, and familiar with many kinds of potatoes. Over the greater portion of the South it is

VEGETABLE GROWING.

necessary to use insecticides and fungicides to raise the largest crop.

VARIETIES.

The earlier varieties are preferable for market, as that is the portion of the crop that pays best. The later varieties will be found good for home use and to give potatoes after the early ones have been exhausted. There are many disadvantages in raising these, however, and often they fail to produce a crop at all, but as the vegetable grower learns more about the requirements of the crop this matter becomes easier. Early Ohio, Early Rose, Beauty of Hebron, Burbank's Seedling are good early varieties. Carman, No. 1, and Rural New York, No. 2, are good later varieties.

SECOND CROP.

It is a common practice to import potatoes for fall and winter use, but this has been proven unnecessary by the production of a second crop. The first crop does not keep well without special care later than September. In July or August tubers are spread out to the light under an arbor or on a barn floor where the sun will not hurt them. This is not necessary, but it will hasten their sprouting, and it is easier to take care of them here than when planted in a field. When the tubers have sprouted well they may be cut and planted, care being taken, of course, not to knock the sprouts off. Sometimes draws are taken off, like from sweet potatoes.

The field may be planted any time, even as late as in September, with a reasonable hope of securing a small crop. It will be found difficult to keep the vines healthy and the field free from weeds. It is also necessary to have the field better prepared for draining; while the potato desires a moist soil it cannot stand a soggy one.

The second crop is simply intended for home use and for local markets. It is well worth the time and trouble to raise this fall crop when one has to pay $1.50 to $2 a bushel at retail for potatoes grown in the North.

JERUSALEM ARTICHOKE.

(HELIANTHUS TUBEROSUS.)

This plant is a native of Brazil and other tropical American countries. Like the Irish potato, it is grown for its under-ground tuber. It was thought at the time of its introduction to cultivation that it would supersede the Irish potato, but it has not proven even a noteworthy rival. Some people are fond of its particular flavor, but others find it distasteful. As a flavoring material it meets with greater favor in this country. Its nutritive ratio is about equal to that of the Irish potato.

Several successful experiments have been made with it in connection with swine feeding, but other crops which give a greater return for labor expended can be raised so easily that this one will not obtain general favor.

The seed may be obtained from the seedsmen and comes in the form of tubers; these are dropped in the soil much as potatoes. Rows are made three to four feet apart and the tubers planted a foot apart in the row. The cultivation is about the same as for ordinary field crops. As soon as the tubers become firm and large in the fall they may be used for cooking, and will be in good condition until they begin to sprout, in the spring. The harvesting may be done by plowing out the row and then picking the tubers up that are in sight. A harrow is then run over the furrow to drag out as many more as is practicable. Hogs may then be turned into the field to gather what is left. If they are not left in the field too long, tubers enough will be left to produce plants for another year, but these will not be in rows, so they cannot be cultivated as the year before. This difficulty may be avoided by saving seed enough to plant the field again.

CHUFA.

This product is known by several other names, but this seems to be the one in general use. The term "ground-nut" is also often applied, and it is sometimes called "nut grass," but both of these terms are used for other vegetables than this one, and the term chufa is restricted to this particular species, consequently we consider this the best of the names. The "seed" of this consists of a tuber which is formed quite deeply under ground, consequently it is not very easy to harvest. These "nuts" (tubers) have a meaty or nutty flavor and are usually quite hard, and are eaten out of the hand like peanuts. Their value lies, however, in their fattening qualities when hogs are turned upon the field, and this is about the only profitable way in which they can be used.

Make the rows about three feet apart, and drop one or two of these tubers to the foot. When the plants appear above the ground they look very much like grass, but more nearly like our common sedge or nutgrass. This plant will be found adapted to any moderately warm soil. The cultivation is very simple, being just such as is given the ordinary field crops, as cow peas or peanuts.

When they have become full grown, and when the frost has killed the herbage, they may be gathered by plowing down the row and picking up those that are in sight. The greater part of the tubers will usually cling to the plant, consequently they can be gathered by simply picking up the plant and shaking the dirt from it. Usually there will be seed enough left in the field to plant it for the next year, but this is too uncertain, so the seed should be saved and planted at the proper time.

SWEET POTATOES.

This crop is cultivated extensively in the Southern States. It may be grown successfully as far north as Nebraska and Maine, but in these sections it cannot be regarded as more than a garden product.

SOIL.

Nearly all the land in the South is adapted to this crop, but clay soil is not as good as loam. The opinion that rich land is not suitable has general credence somehow, but this is a mistake. It is usually said that this kind of land will make them grow to vine, but it is necessary to have vines in order that we may have starch formed to be placed in the roots. Some of the very best crops have been raised on drained muck land. This plant is so versatile that it is difficult to find land that will not produce a fair crop. To produce a large crop, warm sandy soil should be chosen and this well fertilized and plowed deeply. A finer grade for table use may be produced by plowing shallow and using less fertilizer or none at all.

PROPAGATION.

To obtain sets, the whole potatoes should be placed in a hot-bed and covered with an inch of soil, six or seven weeks before the young plants are wanted. By pushing the sets ahead in a hot-bed one will have new potatoes at least a month earlier than by waiting for them to sprout in the field. The early crop will be found to be among the most profitable for shipping; if the crop is wanted for home consumption, it will be sufficient to make a bed in the open from which to obtain slips. In the far North it is necessary to start all plants in a hot-bed. The amount of space required in a hot-bed for a bushel of potatoes varies from nine to thirty-two square feet, depending on the size of the potatoes used.

The number of plants required for an acre varies from 5,000 to 10,000, varying with the locality and the character of the soil.

For repeated drawing, one and a half to two bushels of small roots and four to ten bushels of large ones are required to give sets enough for an acre. Double that quantity will give enough sets at one drawing to plant an acre.

As to the size of roots to choose for growing sets, it is still a doubtful question. As soon as the set is detached from the potato, it can no longer draw on that for nourishment, consequently there is a wide difference between this and the Irish potato. The smaller roots keep easier and produce more sets to the square foot of hot-bed that they occupy, so they are in greater favor among the gardeners of the North. It is probable that the individual root has less influence over the future crop than the parent plant; in other words, small roots from a fine strain are preferable to large roots from a poor one.

Sweet potatoes may be grown from cuttings as well as from sets. There is not sufficient evidence to determine which plan will give the larger yield, but it is quite a saving of material to be able to use cuttings of vines.

This crop may be planted as late as the first of July, but the bulk of it should be in by the first of June.

PREPARATION OF THE LAND AND TRANSPLANTING.

Nearly all of the crop is planted out on ridges, but it is a question whether this is the most desirable method on our land. Experiments in Georgia gave level cultivation an advantage of 9 per cent. in yield, while in Louisiana the ridge culture gave the larger yield. For an extensive crop the plants may be set in checks; this requires fewer plants to an acre and a smaller yield, but it does away with considerable hoeing—an expensive operation.

The labor of transplanting is an important item of expense, and if this could be reduced it would largely increase the acreage. The machine used for transplanting tomatoes may be used for this crop, but hand planting is still adhered to in all sections.

Make the rows three and a half to four feet apart and set the plants fifteen to eighteen inches in the row. If the crop is to be checked make them three and a half by three and a half feet, or for the smaller kinds two and a half by two and a half feet.

CULTIVATION.

The soil should be stirred often enough to keep it loose and free from weeds. If many and heavy rains fall it will be necessary to cultivate oftener than when only a moderate amount of rain falls All cultivation should be shallow and no vines covered. After the vines begin to run it may be necessary to raise them with a pronged hook, or an attachment to the plow.

Such a device may be made of three-eighths inch round iron about four feet long; bend this iron in the shape of a letter J and make a loop or eye at the end of the long arm. It is attached to the plow by passing a half inch bolt through the eye and through the beam of the plow. The short arm of the bent iron is placed down, and by varying the amount of curvature, and having the point more or less sharp, it will run under the vines and raise them out of the way of the plow. A considerable amount of adjusting is necessary to adapt it to the particular plow and to the particular field, but it is certainly a great labor-saving implement.

Among Northern sweet potato growers it is thought that it is detrimental to allow the vines to root, but the idea is not prevalent in the South. Tests on this subject indicate that it will not pay for the trouble, except when cultivation ceases early, or the crop is grown on rich ground, and a heavy rain should fall soon after the last plowing.

FERTILIZER FORMULA.

Nitrogen	4 per cent.
Potash	9 per cent.
Available phosphoric acid	7 per cent.

Use 800 to 1,200 pounds of the above formula. If the soil is rich in nitrogenous matter use less of this element, or if very rich, omit it altogether. If the potatoes are intended for table use the amount of fertilizer should be less than when grown for stock feed or for shipping. Sulphate of potash is preferred as a source of potash. All fertilizers that contain chlorin are said to be detrimental to the quality of the potato, so we should avoid such fertilizers as kainit, muriate of potash and low grade sulphate of potash.

The following quantities of fertilizers will give the amounts of each element called for in the formula.

Element.	Pounds of different material for one acre.
Nitrogen	500 to 800 lbs. cotton-seed meal; or 350 to 500 lbs. dried blood; or 200 to 300 lbs. nitrate of soda; or 150 to 250 lbs. sulphate of ammonia.
Potash	150 to 225 lbs. sulphate of potash; 200 to 300 lbs. nitrate* of potash; or 500 to 700 lbs. cotton-seed hull ashes.
Phosphoric acid	550 to 800 lbs. acid phosphate; or 500 to 700 lbs. dissolved bone.

*Nitrate of potash contains 13 to 14 per cent. nitrogen, so if it is used only one-fourth of the amount of material directed to supply nitrogen should be added—*e. g.*, add only 125 to 200 pounds of cotton-seed meal.

STORING.

The harvesting of this crop is a simple operation; the vines being removed, a man plows the crop out with a large two horse plow. It is necessary to set it deep enough and to have one wide enough to turn the hills out completely; a small plow and a shallow furrow cuts too many potatoes. In sandy loam there is very little left to do else than to pick up the crop.

The storing may be done in houses or banks. A sweet potato house may be built of logs; the cracks daubed with clay mud. The temperature should remain as low as possible without freezing; there are only occasional days when it will be cold enough to do this, but as they are liable to occur every winter, one must prepare for them as well as though they occurred more frequently.

Select a dry place, as handy and as safe as possible; if the spot does not shed water make a bed of cornstalks about eight feet wide and as long as desired. Pile the potatoes on this bed in an A-shaped pile about six feet high. Pack this pile with corn-stalks, rice, straw, or boards may be used. Cover this with loam to the depth of four or six inches. If straw is used, a layer should be packed around the base of the pile, then another higher up, and so on; this will cause it to turn water out. In banking the soil, the same method should be followed. A number of ventilators should be made of boards. Perforate these with augur-holes, and have them run through the central portion of the heap. Fix so that the rain cannot enter through them.

A small quantity may be kept by placing them in dry sand or dry cotton-seed hull and keeping in a cool place. These methods may be used to keep them over from the time of taking them out of the bank until new ones come on. The cooler the storage of sweet potatoes without freezing the better they will keep. Just after they are put into piles there will be a period of sweating; during this time the temperature is liable to run up to 80° F., but no trouble need be anticipated from this source.

VARIETIES.

The varieties that give a very large yield do not make, as a rule, good table potatoes, so we might as well make two general classes—those used for stock, and those for table use. Six most productive varieties tested at the Louisiana Experiment Station are as follow:

Providence	1,072	bushels per acre.
Shanghai	758	" " "
Red Nansemond..	717	" " "
Peabody	696	" " "
Norton	654	" " "
Hyman	651	" " "

These are the highest yields for the year 1893, but it should be mentioned that in the same tests some varieties yielded less than 200 bushels per acre.

As a rule, the Southern consumer prefers a sugary potato, while the Northern people usually prefer a starchy one. Sugar yam, Spanish yam, Yellow yam, Barabadoes, Georgia yam, Hyman, Vineless, and Pumpkin yam are the favorite table varieties for the South. Yellow Nansemond and Jersey are standard varieties for the North. Other varieties that may be recommended for shipping to Northern markets are, Early Carolina, Red Nose, Strasburg, Southern Queen, and Vineless.

There are about a hundred varieties, or about that many different names occur for varieties. The term Yam should be omitted whenever practicable, as this refers to an entirely different vegetable. It will undoubtedly pay to raise some mealy, early varieties for shipping. These always bring a good price in the Northern markets, but are usually a home-grown product, because the Southern varieties are not shipped in.

USES.

Evaporated sweet potatoes were exhibited from Japan at the Columbian Exposition. They are prepared by slicing and drying in the sun (in an evaporator would be better). For the table, they are prepared by soaking and then baking.

In 1893, a factory in Mississippi canned 1000 bushels; the potatoes were bought for 40 cents a bushel and sold for 95 cents a dozen cans of three pounds each; a bushel will make fifteen such cans. The undertaking is certainly to be commended, and ought to be tried throughout our section, in connection with the early vegetables.

One of the most promising uses is to feed to stock. "Three pounds of sweet potatoes afford as much dry matter, quite as much carbonaceous material, but less than half as much protein as is contained in one pound of corn. By using one pound of cotton-seed meal or one pound of cow-peas (seed) for every ten pounds of sweet potatoes, this deficiency of protein is supplied. We can find no digestion experiments with sweet potatoes." The vines may be used for hay, and as such are nearly equal to cow-pea vines.

COST OF PRODUCTION.

Data was collected and a compilation made to ascertain the cost of producing an acre of this crop. The results given were as follows: "Seed potatoes. $1.25 to $4.75; preparation of the land, $1.25 to $4.50; transplanting, $1 (doubtless for vine-cutting) to $6;

horse cultivation, $1 to $3; hoeing, etc., 50 cents to $3.50, and harvesting, $3 to $8." We may say that the approximate cost to produce an acre is $17, not including fertilizer, which is very often not applied, but it is as profitable in this case as with other crops. The cost of producing and harvesting a bushel is placed at from 7 cents to 20 cents, varying with the individual farmers and with the fertility of the soil.

POINTS TO BE IMPROVED UPON.

1. Produce an early crop to bring money when vegetables are out of season. 2. Do away with hoeing. 3. Lessen the cost of tilling by using a two-horse cultivator. 4. Increase the yield by extra cultivation and judicious fertilizing. 5. Decrease the cost of harvesting by using a modified Irish potato digger. 6. If you raise vegetables and sweet potatoes on the same piece of land, use more fertilizer.

YAM.

There are many species of the genus *Discorea* that are known by the name Yam. The more common ones met in the South are the Chinese and Cuban Yam. At one time it was thought that this vegetable would replace both the Irish and the sweet potatoes, but it has not made serious inroads on the popularity of either. The young Chinese yam, when cooked, is very much like the Irish potato in look and taste.

The mode of propagation is by the aerial tubers that form on the vine. These are placed in the ground where the plant is to grow. The crop is allowed to remain in the same place for a number of years—the product being dug as wanted.

The plant sends a very large fleshy root down deeply in the soil. This root continues to be a store-house of nourishment from year to year. The vines may be trained on low trellises or allowed to climb over arbors. In the case of the Cuban species the aerial tubers grow large enough to be used for food ; it is prepared in the same way as potatoes.

If the plants are to be in a solid block, make the rows six or eight feet apart, and plant the tubers about two feet in the row. A low trellis of saplings can be prepared easily. Such a field is said to give food all the year round ; all that is necessary is to go and dig it. It will be necessary to keep the weeds down the first year and to give the vines a good start.

RADISH.

This is one of the most easily grown vegetables that we have. The early varieties mature in an incredibly short time and under a low temperature. In fact, it is so easily grown that there is no profit in raising it for distant markets. A bed 6 x 12 feet can keep a family supplied with this vegetable throughout the entire season for the crop. For local markets this is a favorite crop with the market gardeners; it grows rapidly, costs little, and sells well.

SOIL AND PREPARATION.

Choose a light, warm and rich soil. Water is needed in abundance, but the land must not be soggy. The particles that go to make up the soil should be rather coarser than for the average garden crop.

Remove all rubbish and stir to a moderate depth. Rake the land off smooth, and see that no rough and undecomposed material remains on the plot.

FERTILIZER FORMULA.

Nitrogen .... 3 per cent.
Potash .... 9 per cent.
Available phosphoric acid ..... 7 per cent.

Use 700 to 1000 pounds of the above formula to the acre.

Apply in the drill and work in shallow for the early spring, but deep for the summer or winter radish.

The following will give the amounts of fertilizer to apply to secure the desired quantity of each element:

Element.	Pounds of different material for one acre.
Nitrogen	350 to 500 lbs. cotton-seed meal; or 200 to 300 lbs. dried blood; or 130 to 200 lbs. nitrate of soda; or 100 to 150 lbs. sulphate of ammonia.
Potash	900 to 1300 lbs. kainit; or 120 to 180 lbs. muriate of potash; or 125 to 200 lbs. sulphate of potash; or 230 to 340 lbs. sulphate of potash and sulphate of magnesia.
Phosphoric acid	500 to 700 lbs. acid phosphate; or 400 to 600 lbs. dissolved bone.

VARIETIES.

There are a great many varieties or so-called varieties of radishes. Many of them differ imperceptibly from one another. Among the early spring forms, we have French Breakfast, Scarlet Globe, and Early Scarlet, as good varieties. For the South, the varieties that grow larger and for which more time is required are better. Among this class we have Long Scarlet, Short Top, Chartier (see Fig. 32), Glass, Large White Summer and Large Yellow Summer as good varieties.

The scarlet varieties usually sell better than the white or yellow ones, but for home use there is probably no choice.

The winter varieties grow larger and require much more time for growth. These are favorites in the South, especially the scarlet varieties. For marketing the following are good: White Spanish, Scarlet China, and Celestial. The Long Black Spanish and Round Black Spanish are good in some markets and for home use.

SOWING AND CULTIVATING.

The early varieties should be sown in very rich warm loam four or six weeks before they are wanted. A cold frame is to be recommended. Sow the seed in drills about three inches apart, and drop the seed an inch apart in the row. Cover the seed about a half inch deep. Do not allow the soil to become dry from the time the seed is sown; it is liable to make the radishes pithy.

Only a slight amount of cultivation is required. Weeds may be kept down by pulling as they appear.

The varieties may be cultivated in the open garden also, but as they are wanted for table tit-bits and not for market (in this section) we give them room in the cold frame.

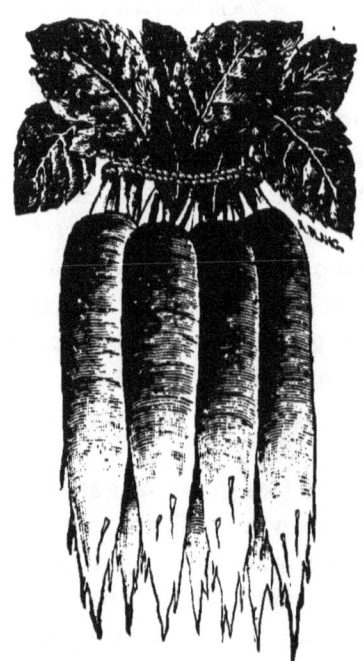

FIG. 32.

Figure 32 represents a bunch of Chartier radish as they are prepared for local markets. The bunching for distant markets is about the same except that most of the foliage is removed.

The summer varieties should be sown in drills twelve to eighteen inches apart, and about an inch apart in the row. Cover the seed about an inch deep.

Stir the soil about twice as often as for ordinary crops.

It sometimes happens that the plants come to a standstill in growth; in such a case, some liquid manure should be applied along the row.

Make the rows, for winter varieties, about eighteen inches apart and thin out to about two inches in the row. These varieties require a long time to mature, so they should be sown in November, or December; some may be sown as early as in October.

The cultivation is the same as for summer radish.

MARKETING.

The bunches are made about four inches in diameter (see Fig. 32). The roots are washed clean of all adhering soil, and are turned up so as to show the clear scarlet and white color. Radishes make a fine display for marketing. For distant market they are packed in crates or barrels to suit the convenience of the shipper.

SEED RAISING.

A variety that grows well on a particular soil and sells well in the market ought to be grown to seed by the gardener. Select the finest radishes and allow these to remain in the place where they were grown. As soon as the flowering stalk has reached a height of eighteen inches, a strong stake should be driven down beside the radish and the seed stalk tied to this. Care is necessary to remove the stalks as they ripen or birds are liable to become troublesome. Hang the stalks up away from mice and rats, and when all are dry the seed may be beaten out. Remove as much of the large stalks as you can handily and place the pods in a large sack. After beating, the seed may be winnowed out and placed away for seeding time.

BEET.

This vegetable has not been grown extensively in the South, but as the transportation becomes cheaper and better, this crop will increase in favor. At this time there are few Florida grown beets on the New York market. They never bring an extra fine price, but the market gardeners of the South must learn to economize and be able to raise standard vegetables at close margins. We are rapidly approaching the condition when high prices for vegetables will be a thing of the past. Beets ship well and are always in demand by the laboring and mercantile classes, hence they are rarely a complete loss. Another consideration is that they make excellent feed for stock.

SOIL AND PREPARATION.

Beets want a moist and rather heavy soil. One that would be considered too damp for the usual garden crops will raise a good crop of beets; of course, a cold, clammy soil should be avoided. Drained land makes an excellent beet field, provided the amount of nitrogen in it is comparatively small.

The land should be plowed deeply and harrowed level.

FERTILIZER FORMULA.

Nitrogen ... ... 4 per cent.
Potash ... ... 9 per cent.
Available phosphoric acid .... 6 per cent.

Use 600 to 1000 pounds of the above formula to an acre.

When beets are raised for sugar, sulphate of potash, free from chlorin, is used as a source of potash.

The following ingredients will give the desired amounts of each element for one acre:

Element.	Pounds of different material for one acre.
Nitrogen	400 to 650 lbs. cotton-seed meal; or 250 to 400 lbs. dried blood; or 160 to 275 lbs. nitrate of soda; or 130 to 200 lbs. sulphate of ammonia.
Potash	800 to 1,300 lbs. kainit; or 100 to 180 lbs. muriate of potash; or 110 to 190 lbs. sulphate of potash; or 200 to 350 lbs. sulphate of potash and sulphate of magnesia.
Phosphoric acid	360 to 600 lbs. acid phosphate; or 300 to 500 lbs. dissolved bone.

The fertilizer should be applied along the row and worked in thoroughly a week or ten days before the seed is planted.

VARIETIES.

Extra Early Bastian (see Fig. 33) is one of the best early beets. It has the disadvantage of becoming stringy, if a dry spell occurs, if it matures or if allowed to stand too long. Eclipse and Extra Early Egyptian are also good for shipping. As a rule, the turnip-shaped varieties are preferred in the northern markets; as to color, the market prefers a deep red.

There are many other varieties worthy of mention, and desirable for home use.

The varieties used for making sugar, and for feeding to stock, are large and coarse grained, consequently, not valuable for a garden crop.

SEEDING AND CULTIVATING.

Make the rows eighteen inches or two feet apart. Sow the seed about three times as thick as you want the plants to stand. While the seed rarely fails, it does not come up evenly, so we sow it very thick, and cut out to make a good stand. Seeding is best done by drill. When the plants are about an inch high, thin out to about three inches apart in the row. If the land is strong, two rows may be drilled, about four inches apart, to make one row, or if the seed is sown by hand, make a drill about five inches wide and scatter the seed along this. Cover the seed from a half to an inch deep, depending on the soil and moisture.

Soon after the seedlings are up, there is a considerable period during which they make no apparent progress, especially if the weather is unfavorable. If the temperature is at the freezing point, it is well not to force the plantlets; but during warm weather an application of liquid manure or a solution of nitrate of soda will hasten them over this condition.

Cultivating should all be done with a wheel-hoe or a horse; avoid using a hand hoe—it is slow and expensive. The soil should be kept loose, so the fleshy roots can form in the ground. As the tap root goes down straight and deep, there is no danger of disturbing it while cultivating.

It is usually unprofitable to transpant this crop for the market; hence, do not practice it, except when you know the product will sell well, or for home use.

Fig. 33.

MARKETING.

Beets may be marketed as soon as they are two or

more inches across. They should be pulled and the leaves cut an inch or less from the fleshy root. If the leaves are cut too close, it causes the roots to lose more moisture than they otherwise would, and hence appear in the market wilted. (For way of cutting leaves see Fig. 33).

The ordinary vegetable crate will be found desirable to use for marketing, although barrels and large boxes are often used.

In the vicinity of a pickling establishment small beets may be raised, or the thinning out may be delayed until the roots can be used for pickling.

TURNIP.

This crop is so easily grown that it is scarcely necessary to discuss it from that point of view, yet it is not appreciated as it ought to be. The winters in the South are not cold enough to freeze this vegetable, so it can be on the table for several months in the winter, and until quite late into spring. As every vegetable-grower ought to raise his own butter and milk, he will find that half an acre of the largest varieties of turnips will add surprisingly to the quantity of these dairy products he is able to produce.

Turnips cannot be recommended as a crop to be shipped to distant markets, but the local markets and Southern cities will use a considerable quantity.

SOIL AND PREPARATION.

Newly prepared, or what is often called raw land, will raise a crop, if it is not too badly stocked with weeds. Muck land or land containing much nitrogenous matter should be avoided, except in cases where the product is to be used for stock feed. Wet or soggy land will not raise a crop, but, on the whole, this crop has a much wider range in the matter of soil and moisture than the majority of cultivated plants.

Plow deeply if the land is heavy or inclined to be hard, but a light loam will need but a slight amount of stirring.

FERTILIZER FORMULA.

Nitrogen .... 3 per cent.
Potash .... 8 per cent.
Available phosphoric acid ... 8 per cent.

If the land is rich in nitrogenous matter, the nitrogen of the above formula may be omitted. Use 500 to 800 pounds in the drill.

TURNIP.

The following amounts of fertilizers will give as much of each element as is desired for one acre.

Element.	Pounds of different material for one acre.
Nitrogen	⎧ 250 to 400 lbs. cotton-seed meal; or ⎨ 150 to 240 lbs. dried blood; or ⎩ 100 to 160 lbs. nitrate of soda; or 80 to 125 lbs. sulphate of ammonia.
Potash	⎧ 500 to 800 lbs. kainit; or ⎨ 80 to 125 lbs. nitrate of potash; or ⎨ 80 to 125 lbs. sulphate of potash; or ⎩ 150 to 240 lbs. sulphate of potash and sulphate of magnesia.
Phosphoric acid	⎧ 400 to 650 lbs. acid phosphate; or ⎩ 350 to 550 lbs. dissolved bone.

FIG. 34.

VARIETIES.

The field varieties may be used in the kitchen if taken before they mature. After they are quite grown they become too coarse grained; this may be changed somewhat by withholding the nitrogen in the fertilizer we use. Early Flat Dutch (see Fig. 34) is an old and standard variety. Scarlet Kashmyr is a good early variety for quick growing. Early White Egg is also good for an early crop. Large White French (Sweet German) is good for field planting. Golden Ball and Yellow Globe make a good large crop also.

PLANTING AND CULTIVATING.

Turnip seeds are best sown with a seed drill. They may be sown by hand, but this is not satisfactory. A tin can, with a hole punched in the bottom, may be used with more or less aggravation.

Make the rows eighteen inches or two feet apart, and sow the seed about twice as thick as you want the plants to stand. Cover the seed one-half inch to an inch deep. When the plants are four or five inches high, thin out so as to give the plants from four to eight inches each.

The cultivation needs to be sufficient to keep the ground mellow and the weeds from growing.

MARKETING.

Turnips that can be marketed in October and November meet with ready sale in local markets, in bunches containing five to eight turnips and "greens." Later, the greens are not wanted, and they are marketed like potatoes.

RUTA BAGA.

This vegetable (see Fig. 35), is also called the Swedish Turnip. There are only a few points in which it differs from the turnip. The roots can stand the long summer heat without becoming acrid or woody, and while they cannot be considered a delicate dish, they fill an important gap that otherwise would occur in the kitchen garden of the South.

For a summer crop the seed should be sown in winter or spring.

For other points regarding this crop, the reader is referred to the turnip.

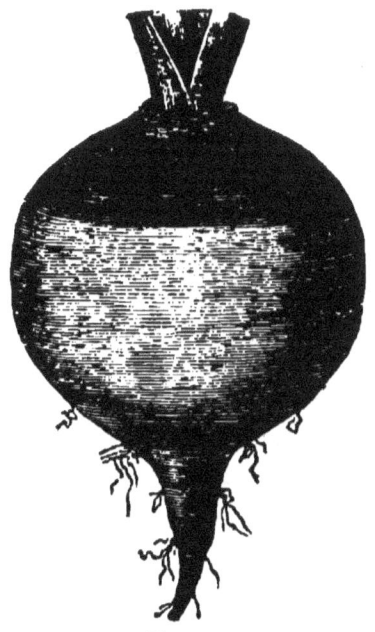

FIG. 35.

CARROT.

This root crop may be shipped to a distant market without danger of loss, but there is very little, if any, profit in it at present. Vegetable growers should raise and ship a few crates during April and May. It is also an excellent crop to raise for home use. The nutritive ratio is high for vegetables and its taste pleasant. If one has planted more than is needed, they may be fed to horses, cows, or hogs to good advantage. In many European countries they are raised for this purpose; butter from carrot fed milch cows has a pleasant odor, sweet taste and a fine, yellow color.

The vegetable is a good keeper, so the Northern markets are stocked with the old crop until growing season in the spring—April or May. New carrots may be found in the New York markets, however, during the late winter months.

SOIL AND PREPARATION.

A deep, rich, dark-colored loam is usually chosen for this crop when grown extensively. It will make good roots on a sandy loam or even on a light clay soil, but the ground must be mellow. It is not necessary that the land be rich in nitrogenous matter, but should contain a good supply of phosphoric acid and potash. A damp or wet soil will not raise a good crop.

Plow the land deeply and remove all rubbish, especially undecomposed vegetable matter.

FERTILIZER FORMULA.

Nitrogen .. .. 3 per cent.
Potash. ....8 per cent.
Available phosphoric acid..... 7 per cent.

Use from 600 to 900 pounds of the above formula on

ordinary land. If the land is rich in nitrogenous matter, use less nitrogen, or omit altogether from land strong in nitrogen.

Mix the fertilizer thoroughly with the soil and see to it that it is worked in deeper than usual.

The following table gives the number of pounds of fertilizer per acre to obtain the requisite amount of each element:

Element.	Pounds of different material for one acre.
Nitrogen	300 to 450 lbs. cotton-seed meal; or 180 to 270 lbs. dried blood; or 120 to 180 lbs. nitrate of soda; or 100 to 150 lbs. sulphate of ammonia.
Potash	600 to 900 lbs. kainit; or 100 to 150 lbs. muriate of potash; or 100 to 150 lbs. sulphate of potash; or 200 to 300 lbs. sulphate of potash, and sulphate of ammonia.
Phosphoric acid.	425 to 650 lbs. acid phosphate; or 350 to 525 lbs. dissolved bone.

FIG. 36.

VARIETIES.

Early Scarlet Horn, Short Horn, Half Long Nantes are favorites (see Fig. 36), orange colored and early, and doubtless best for our section. Long Orange and Large White Belgian will prove more vigorous, and are generally grown for stock feed; so should not be sown in the market garden except when there are facilities for marketing the half grown crop.

SOWING AND CULTIVATING.

Sow the seed with a drill, in rows about eighteen inches apart. Cover the seed about half an inch deep. Sow about three times as many seed as you want plants, and when the plants are an inch high, trim out the inferior ones, leaving the others to stand from two to four inches in the row.

The time of sowing will depend upon the variety in hand. The later and longer ones should be sown in October, the earlier ones in November, and the very earliest ones about the first of December. The seed is quite slow to germinate, so a few seeds of cabbage, radish, or turnips should be mixed with it to indicate the row before the carrot seedlings are visible.

The soil should be kept in a high state of cultivation, so plowing should begin before the seed is up. Plow deeply and close to the rows, except during dry weather, when plowing should be shallow and often enough to keep the land mellow and plenty of air in the soil.

MARKETING.

The young or spring crop is marketed with the greens; this is mainly for convenience. The carrots are washed, the dry and large leaves removed, and about six tied in a bunch. Marketing is usually done in boxes or barrels, but good crates would be preferable.

PARSNIPS.

Many people are delighted with the taste of parsnips from the first trial; others acquire a liking for them, while only a very few people do not relish them.

We would not advise gardeners to use them for stock feed, though it is often done.

It is not a good vegetable to be grown for distant markets, but should be raised for home use and local markets.

SOIL AND PREPARATION.

Its native habitat is in moist or swampy places, but here it grows "all to top" and produces only a small root, but with the transfer to dry uplands comes an increased size of root.

Select a dry, deep loam, and prepare as deeply as your implements and soil will permit: work the fertilizer in deep.

FERTILIZER FORMULA.

Nitrogen.................................. 3 per cent.
Potash .... 8 per cent.
Available phosphoric acid.....9 per cent.

Use from 600 to 900 pounds of the above formula in the drills. Be sure that it is worked in deeply and thoroughly. A good way will be to run out a deep double furrow where the row is to be, apply a portion of the fertilizer, and mix thoroughly with enough soil to fill about one-third of the furrow; then add some more fertilizer and mix in more soil; continue this mixing until all the fertilizer has been used, when the row should be a little above the general level. If the flat or turnip-shaped varieties are planted, the preparation and fertilizer need not be so deep.

The following table will give the amount of fertilizers to use for one acre to secure the desired quantity of each element:

Element.	Pounds of different material for one acre.
Nitrogen	300 to 450 lbs. cotton-seed meal; or 180 to 270 lbs. dried blood; or 120 to 180 lbs. nitrate of soda; or 100 to 150 lbs. sulphate of ammonia.
Potash	600 to 900 lbs. kainit; or 100 to 150 lbs. muriate of potash; or 100 to 150 lbs. sulphate of potash; or 200 to 300 lbs. sulphate of potash and sulphate of magnesia.
Phosphoric acid	550 to 800 lbs. acid phosphate; or 450 to 700 lbs. dissolved bone.

VARIETIES.

Fig. 37.

The Hollow Crown and Student (see Fig. 37) are good, long varieties; the first named is the larger and longer. A shorter variety is Maltese, but the first two meet with greater favor.

SOWING AND CULTIVATING.

Sow during September, October and November. The earliest sowing will allow the plants to mature by the first of January. The summer crop has not met with as much success. There is no danger of the young plants being frozen. Make the rows eighteen inches or two feet apart and thin to four inches in the row. The seed is a little slow to germinate, so it will be well to add some radish or turnip seed to mark the row.

The cultivation is best carried on by horse after the plants are about four or five inches high.

When the roots are about a foot long and an inch in diameter, they will be found sufficiently mature to use.

Parsnips are marketed in bulk, very much as potatoes.

The preparation for table use is quite similar to that of potatoes.

SALSIFY.

The demand for this, the vegetable oyster, is continually increasing. While it will not be in great demand for home consumption, it is still a good plant to raise, as it sells readily and can stand shipping. The seed is difficult to save on account of birds destroying it.

This seed should be sown in the fall or during the winter. The cultivation and preparation of the soil is similar to that for the usual root crops. A sandy loam is preferred. The rows are sown about two feet apart and the plants thinned to four or six inches in the row.

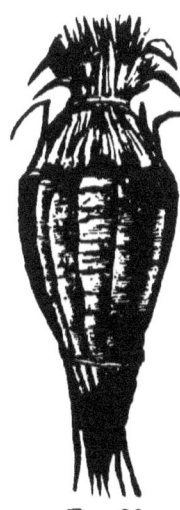

Fig. 38.

For market the large tap root is dug up and that with the leaves is washed and trimmed (see Fig. 38.) Six or eight usually make a bunch. In the North it is planted in the spring (May) and dug in October. The care after digging is about like that given to celery. It is used mostly during the winter and early spring. A good market for this vegetable can be opened by growing it so it can be offered for sale during May and June, after the fresh oyster can no longer be obtained.

FERTILIZER FORMULA.

Nitrogen .... 3 per cent.
Potash .... 8 per cent.
Available phosphoric acid ...... 9 per cent.

Use 800 to 1,200 pounds to the acre; work in thoroughly and deeply.

HORSE RADISH.

This plant has not been grown to a large extent in the South. It requires a deep, rich, sandy soil, and is usually planted as a by crop.

It is well worthy of a good test in each locality, but no one should invest in this crop without having a personal knowledge that it will succeed.

Prepare the soil as for cabbage.

The sets will be found to be small straight roots, about half an inch in diameter and six inches long. Make the rows about two feet apart and plant the sets eighteen inches in the row. Make a deep hole with a dibber, or other suitable implement, and drop the set in it in an upright position. The crown of the set should go from two to four inches below the surface of the soil.

The cultivation need not be frequent, but had best be deep.

FERTILIZER FORMULA.

Nitrogen.. .... 4 per cent.
Potash .... 10 per cent.
Available phosphoric acid..... 7 per cent.

Use about 600 pounds per acre in the row.

The roots are the only marketable portions; these should be removed from the soil, washed and trimmed. The roots will remain in a marketable condition for several weeks after digging, and may be shipped as freight.

INDEX.

A.

	PAGE.
Acre, Number of Plants per	41
Artichoke, Globe	129
Artichoke, Jerusalem	215
Asparagus	51
Blanching	54
Bunching and Crating	53
Canning	55
Crating, Bunching and	53
Cutting	52
Fertilizer	56
Marketing	53
Planting	52
Plants, Raising	54
Preparation of the Plot	51
Raising Plants	54
Varieties	55

B.

Bean (Bush)	192
Cultivating, planting and	194
Fertilizer	193
Harvesting	195
Market, Preparing for	195
Planting and Cultivating	194
Soil	193
Varieties	193
Bean (Pole)	196
Varieties	197
Beet	230
Cultivating, Seeding and	231
Fertilizer	230
Marketing	232
Seeding and Cultivating	231
Soil and Preparation	230
Varieties	231
Borecole, Kale	71
Brocoli	97

C.

	PAGE.
Cabbage	86
Bed, Plant	86
Cultivating, Planting and	89
Fertilizer Amounts	89
Fertilizer Formula	89
Market, Preparing for	90
Marketing	90
Plant Bed	86
Planting and Cultivating	89
Seed, Sowing the	87
Soil	88
Sowing the Seed	87
Varieties	87
Canteloupe. See Musk Melon.	
Carrot	238
Cultivating, Sowing and	240
Fertilizer	238
Marketing	240
Soil and Preparation	238
Sowing and Cultivating	240
Varieties	239
Cauliflower	92
Cultivation	94
Crating	95
Cutting	94
Fertilizer Formula	96
Seed Sowing	92
Setting Out	94
Soil	94
Varieties	96
Celeriac	85
Celery	72
Culture, The New Celery	78
Fertilizer Formula	84
Fertilizer Amount	84
Irrigation	80
Marketing	81
Market, Preparing for	82
Seed Sowing	74

	PAGE.
Celery—Continued.	
Soil	72
Soil, Preparation of the	72
Transplanting	75
Varieties	84
Chicory	67
Chives	117
Chufa	216
Cold Frame, Preparing a	36
Compost	10
Collards	99
Fertilizer Formula	99
Crate, How to Make a	46
Cress	127
Crops, Rotation of	21
Cucumbers	167
Cultivation	169
Fertilizer	173
Picking and Packing	170
Seed Saving	171
Soil and Preparation of the Field	168
Varieties	173

E.

Egg Plant	150
Cold Frame, Hot Bed and	151
Cultivation	155
Fertilizer Formula	154
Flower-Pots, Using	152
Gathering	155
Hot Bed and Cold Frames	151
Marketing	156
Pots, Using Flower	152
Preparation, Soil and	153
Seed Saving	156
Soil and Preparation	153
Varieties	151
Endive	65
Fertilizer Formula	66
English Pea	190
Fertilizer Amounts	191
Fertilizer Formula	191

F.

	PAGE.
Fertilizer, Amounts of, How to Compute in a Given Formula	15
Fertilizer Elements, Per Cents. of	14
Fertilizer, Commercial	5
Sources of Nitrogen	8, 17
Sources of Phosphoric Acid	5
Sources of Potash	7
Fertilizing, What is	4
(See also Manure.)	
Field, How to Test	19

G.

Garlic	117
Gherkins	178
Globe Artichoke	129
Goober	205
Gourd	189

H.

Horse Radish	244
Hot Beds	32
Construction	33
Selection of a Location	32
Using the Manure	34
How to Test a Field	19
How to Test the Vitality of Seed	27

I.

Irish Potato	206
Crop, Second	214
Cultivating	211
Fertilizer	210
Fertilizer Amounts	211
Fertilizer Formula	210
General Remarks	213
Harvesting	212
Planting	209
Remarks, General	213
Second Crop	214

Irish Potato—Continued.

	PAGE.
Seed	208
Soil and Preparation	206
Storing	213
Varieties	214

J.

Jerusalem Artichoke ... 215

K.

Kale. See Borecole.
Kohl-Rabi ... 101

L.

Land, Preparation of the	38
Shall We Plow Deep?	39
Well Drained	38
Well Cleared	39
Leek	115
Fertilizer	116
Lettuce	61
Cultivation	62
Fertilizer Formula	63
Fertilizer, Amounts to Use	63
Marketing	64
Plant Bed	61
Preparing Field	62
Raising Seed	64
Varieties	63
Location, Selection of, for Hot Bed	32

M.

Machine, How to Test a	29
Manure	9
Using the Manure (in Hot Bed)	34
Marketing	44
How to Make a Crate	46
The Packing House	44
Melon, Musk. See Musk Melon.	
Melon, Water. See Water Melon.	
Muck	13

250   INDEX.

	PAGE.
Mushrooms	48
Preparation of Bed	49
Musk Melons	175
Cultivating, Planting and	176
Fertilizer	176
Marketing	177
Planting and Cultivating	176
Seed, Saving	177
Soil and Preparation	175
Varieties	175

N.

Nasturtiums	128
Nitrogen	8
Nitrogen, Plants as a Source of	17
Nutmeg Melon. See Musk Melon.	

O.

Onion	102
Crating	111
Cultivation	107
Curing the Crop	110
Fertilizing	104
Fertilizer Amounts	105
Fertilizer Formula	105
Old Plan, The	109
Preparing the Land	102
Raising Onions from Sets	111
Resumé,	113
Seed	103
Seed Bed	103
Setting Out	105
Soil	102
Time to Sow	104
Varieties,	111
Okra	164
Varieties	164
Fertilizer Formula	165

P.

	PAGE.
Packing House	44
Parsley	125
Varieties	126
Parsnip	241
Cultivation, Sowing and	242
Fertilizer	241
Soil and Preparation	241
Sowing and Cultivating	242
Varieties	242
Pea, English. See English Pea.	
Peanut	198
Cultivating	200
Fertilizer	204
Harvesting	201
Planting	199
Soil and Preparation	198
Varieties	203
Peppers	159
Cold Frames, Hot Beds and	160
Cultivation	162
Fertilizer Amounts	163
Fertilizer Formula	163
Hot Beds and Cold Frames	160
Marketing	162
Seed Saving	163
Soil and Preparation	161
Varieties	160
Phosphoric Acid, Sources of	5
Plants as a Source of Nitrogen	17
Plants Used to Enrich the Soil	17
Plant Bed, Preparation of a	37
Plants per Acre, Number of	41
Potash	7
Potato, Irish. See Irish Potato.	
Potato, Sweet. See Sweet Potato.	
Preparing a Cold Frame	36
Pumpkins	184

R.

	PAGE.
Radish	226
Cultivating, Sowing and	227
Fertilizer	226
Marketing	229
Seed Raising	229
Soil and Preparation	226
Sowing and Cultivating	227
Varieties	227
Ruta Baga	237
Rotation of Crops	21
Rhubarb	57
Cultivation	59
Fertilizer	58
Forcing	60
Marketing	59
Planting	57
Varieties	58

S.

Salsify	243
Seed Growing	26
Seed, How to Test Vitality of	27
Seed, Quantity Required for an Acre	31
Seed Sowing	29
How to Test a Machine	29
Quantity of Seed Required	30
Selecting Varieties	30
Soil	1
Composition of	2
Elements Necessary to Plant Growth	2
Mechanical Classification of	1
Why Land Becomes Poor	3
Spinach	69
Fertilizer Formula	70
Sprouts	91
Squashes	179
Cultivation	182
Fertilizer	180
Marketing	183

Squashes—Continued.	PAGE.
Planting	182
Soil, Selecting the	179
Varieties	181
Swedish Turnip. See Ruta Baga.	
Sweet Potato	217
Cost of Producing	223
Cultivation	219
Fertilizer Amounts	220
Fertilizer Formula	220
Points to be Improved Upon	224
Preparation of the Land and Transplanting	218
Propagation	217
Producing, Cost of	223
Soil	217
Storing	221
Transplanting, Preparation of the Land and	218
Uses,	223
Varieties	222

T.

Tobacco	118
Cultivation	121
Curing	122
Curing Barns	123
Cutting	122
Fertilizer Amounts	120
Fertilizer Formula	120
Hauling	122
Preparation of the Land	121
Raising the Seedlings	118
Seedlings, Raising the	118
Sorting, Stripping and	124
Stripping and Sorting	124
Suckering, Topping and	121
Topping and Suckering	121
Transplanting	120
Varieties	118
Tomato	131
Canning	147
Cold Frames	133

Tomato—Continued.   PAGE.
    Cultivation.. 140
    Fall Crop, Summer and.. 146
    Fertilizer Amounts... 134
    Fertilizer Formula.. 134
    Hot Beds.. 132
    Location, Soil and... 137
    Packing House... 144
    Picking.. 143
    Pruning... 141
    Preparing the Field.. 138
    Saving Seed... 147
    Seed... 135
    Seed Bed... 133
    Seed Saving... 147
    Setting Out.. 139
    Soil and Location.. 137
    Sorting.. 145
    Staking... 142
    Summer and Fall Crop... 146
    Transplanting.. 136
    Trellising.. 142
    Varieties... 134
Transplanting.. 42
Turnip.. 234
    Cultivation and Planting... 236
    Fertilizer.. 234
    Marketing.. 236
    Planting and Cultivation... 236
    Soil and Preparation.. 234
    Varieties... 235
Turnip, Swedish. See Ruta Baga.

V.

Varieties, Selecting.. 30
Vitality of Seed, How to Test.. 27

W.

Water and Watering... 24
Water Cress. See Cress.
Water Melon.. 185
    Cultivation... 187

Watermelon—Continued.
　Fertilizer... 185
　Marketing... 187
　Planting.. 186
　Seed Saving... 188
　Soil.. 185
　Varieties.. 186
Weeds... 23

Y.

Yam.. 225

www.ingramcontent.com/pod-product-compliance
Lightning Source LLC
Chambersburg PA
CBHW032139230426
43672CB00011B/2391